The Genesis of the Naval Profession

The Genesis of the Naval Profession has been compiled by René
Moelker and Stephen Mennell mainly from unpublished typescripts in the Norbert Elias papers at the Deutsches Literaturarchiv, Marbach am Neckar, Germany. It complements, but
is not formally part of, the Collected Works of Norbert Elias,
which are being published in 18 volumes by University College
Dublin Press.

The Collected Works of Norbert Elias

The Genesis of the Naval Profession

NORBERT ELIAS

EDITED AND WITH
AN INTRODUCTION BY
RENÉ MOELKER AND STEPHEN MENNELL

University College Dublin Press
Preas Choláiste Ollscoile Bhaile Átha Cliath

This collection first published 2007 by University College Dublin Press
Norbert Elias's text © Norbert Elias Foundation, Amsterdam, 2007
Introduction and editors' notes © René Moelker and Stephen Mennell,
2007

ISBN 978-1-904558-80-4

University College Dublin Press
Newman House, 86 St Stephen's Green
Dublin 2, Ireland
www.ucdpress.ie

CIP data available
from the British Library

Typeset in France in Ehrhardt by Elaine Burberry
Text design by Lyn Davies
Printed in England on acid-free paper
by Cromwell Press, Trowbridge, Wiltshire

Contents

Norbert Elias
1897–1990

Norbert Elias was one of the great sociologists of our time. Born in 1897, he lived through most of the twentieth century, and found his life radically affected by some of that century's major events. Brought up in a Jewish family in the German *Kaiserreich*, he served as a soldier in the First World War, became a sociologist in the short-lived Weimar Republic, had to flee his country after the National Socialists came to power in 1933, suffered hard times as a refugee in Paris and London, and entered on a university career in England only in his late fifties. Having reached retirement age in 1962, he taught sociology in Ghana for two years, and, after his return to Europe, remained active for more than 25 years writing and teaching in various countries. He died in Amsterdam in 1990, at the age of 93.

Elias's protected youth in the Silesian city of Breslau – then in Germany, now Wrocław in Poland – came to an abrupt end when he enlisted to serve in the German army during the First World War. Following his demobilisation, Elias studied medicine and philosophy at the University of Breslau. He wrote his doctoral thesis in philosophy, graduating in 1924, but not before having become highly critical of what he saw as the philosophers' failure to recognise the importance of the creation and transmission of knowledge as an intergenerational learning process, and ultimately rejecting philosophy as a discipline. The runaway inflation of 1922–3 forced him to take work for a time in business, and when he returned to his studies he chose the nascent discipline of sociology at the University of Heidelberg. He worked under Alfred Weber, Max's brother, but also became associated with the young Karl Mannheim who was establishing his reputation in the sociology of knowledge. In 1930 Mannheim moved to a chair at Frankfurt, and Elias joined him as his

Assistant in the Department of Sociology, members of which shared a milieu with the Marxist 'Frankfurt School' but remained intellectually and organisationally separate.

At Frankfurt, Elias wrote his *Habilitationsschrift* (the thesis that qualified him for a career as a university lecturer in Germany) about courts, courtiers and courtly culture in early modern Europe. Because of the Nazi seizure of state power in Germany early in 1933 this text was to remain unpublished for more than 35 years. Elias fled first to France and then to England. He was interned as an enemy alien for about eight months early in the Second World War, but later became a British citizen. His mother was killed in Auschwitz. During and after the war he earned a meagre living by lecturing to adult education classes. With S. H. Foulkes, a friend from his Frankfurt days, he helped to found Group Analysis, which became an important school of psychotherapy. Finally, in 1954, he was appointed a lecturer, and later Reader, in sociology at the University of Leicester. In 1962–4, after his formal retirement, he went to West Africa as Professor of Sociology at the University of Ghana, a vivid experience for him, in the course of which he acquired a large collection of African art. From the mid-1960s, Elias held Visiting Professorships in Germany and the Netherlands. Between 1978 and 1984 he was a Permanent Fellow-in-Residence at the Zentrum für interdisziplinäre Forschung, Bielefeld. He also made two shorter visits to the USA, giving lectures in New York, Boston, and Bloomington, Indiana. Leicester remained his main home until 1978, when he moved to Amsterdam, where he died on 1 August 1990. International celebrity came to him only towards the end of his long life. In 1977 he was the first recipient of the prestigious Theodor W. Adorno Prize awarded by the city of Frankfurt; in 1988 he was the first winner of the Premio Europeo Amalfi; the Universities of Bielefeld and Strasbourg conferred honorary doctorates on him; and he was honoured with high national decorations by both Germany and the Netherlands.

Elias completed his most famous book, *Über den Prozess der Zivilisation* (now widely known as *The Civilising Process*) during his early years of exile. It was published by an émigré press in Switzerland in 1939. Attracting little attention at the time, its greatness was widely recognised only when it was republished thirty years later. In a poll carried out in 1998 by the International Sociological Association, it was ranked among the ten most important sociological works of the twentieth century. Elias took a lively interest in all aspects of human life, past and present, and continued to develop the theory of civilising processes in many directions. Throughout his life, he elaborated a sociological theory of the growth of knowledge and the sciences. He always sought a secure basis for human knowledge in order to 'steer between the Scylla of philosophical absolutism and the Charybdis of sociological relativism'. He pioneered the sociological study of sport, and wrote insightfully about art and literature. The common thread was always how people's individual emotions and thoughts are embedded in bonds of social interdependence, and change in accordance with long-term changes in the overall structure of these bonds.

Apart from *The Civilising Process*, all of Elias's 15 books and most of his essays were published after he had formally retired. Some of these works were first written in English, some in German. The Collected Works to be published by UCD Press will include all of his printed works, including many never before available in English.

Abbreviations

BJS	*British Journal of Sociology*
Cal. S.P. Dom.	Calendar of State Papers Domestic
Cal. S.P. Ven.	Calendar of State Papers Venetian
DNB	*Dictionary of National Biography*
L.P. (Henry VIII)	Letters and Papers, Foreign and Domestic, of the Reign of Henry VIII
LSE	London School of Economics and Political Science
NE Archive	Norbert Elias papers, Deutsches Literaturarchiv, Marbach am Neckar, Germany
NRS	Navy Records Society
Pub. NRS	Publications of the Navy Records Society

Acts of Parliament are cited, according to convention, by the year of the sovereign's reign and statute book chapter number, as in 13 George II, c.3.

Editors' Preface

This small book is not formally part of the Collected Works of Norbert Elias, which over the next few years are being published in 18 volumes by UCD Press. The reason is that, with very minor exceptions, the Collected Works consist of books and essays that Elias authorised for publication and which found their way into print – whether in English or German – during Elias's lifetime or shortly after his death. In contrast, only about a quarter of *The Genesis of the Naval Profession* has been published before. Elias had hoped to write a book on the subject, but never completed it. The book as it appears now has been reconstructed by the editors from a large number of unfinished typescripts that are lodged among the Elias papers in the Deutsches Literaturarchiv, Marbach am Neckar, Germany. In our Introduction, we explain how we were able to put together a book that, we believe, resembles a shortened version of the book that Elias might have published had he completed his work on the naval profession. We also describe the context and significance of Elias's research, allowing ourselves a little more freedom than is permitted to editors of volumes of the Collected Works to interpret and set in context what he has written.

As editors we have learned a great deal from the studies that we unearthed from the archives. We developed an interest in English maritime history and a taste for tales about privateers, naval warfare and the social relations between the men who sailed the King's ships. The studies make good reading. Some parts, especially the paradigmatic case study of the rivalry between Francis Drake and Thomas Doughty, make a dramatic story. Norbert Elias would have liked to stage that story, for he himself wrote an outline for a play about this breathtaking and dramatic conflict between the mariner and the soldier. It is on file in the archives, and we have included part of it, 'the last act', in chapter 7 of this book. We hope that the reader will share our enthusiasm and will enjoy the studies in the genesis of the naval profession as much as we did.

We wish to thank the Norbert Elias Foundation, the Deutsches Literaturarchiv, and the National University of Ireland for their support. For their help and encouragement we should like to thank Johan Goudsblom, Harry Kirkels, Andrew Linklater, Barbara Mennell, Nicholas Rodger, Joseph Soeters, Keith Thomas and Saskia Visser.

RENÉ MOELKER
STEPHEN MENNELL
Netherlands Defence Academy
University College Dublin

INTRODUCTION

Elias's Studies of the Naval Profession

RENÉ MOELKER AND STEPHEN MENNELL

Footnotes do not normally receive much attention from readers. But it happens that this book arose out of a peculiar footnote at the beginning of Elias's article 'Studies in the genesis of the naval profession', published in 1950 in the *British Journal of Sociology* (*BJS*). The note reads

> This is the first of three studies in the origins and the early development of the career of naval officers in England. ... (p. 134 below)

The note continues with a description of all the three studies that were to be published in the *BJS*. What is peculiar about the footnote is not its presence but the fact that the other two studies were never published in later issues of the *BJS*. Many years later, this aroused René Moelker's curiosity. Whatever happened to the unpublished studies in the genesis of the naval profession? Were they never written? Were they published somewhere else? Were they gathering dust among the Norbert Elias papers in the Deutsches Literaturarchiv in Marbach am Neckar in Germany? And did the *BJS* decide not to publish the other two studies? If so, why? More and more questions demanded answers. It became something of a quest – a quest pursued by René Moelker in the Norbert Elias Archive in Marbach am Neckar. In this Introduction,[1] we describe the unpublished studies, and place Elias's studies of the genesis of the naval profession in the context of his own writings, of military sociology, and more broadly of sociology as a discipline.

It was not expected initially that Elias's unpublished studies in the genesis of the naval profession would form a coherent whole. To our surprise they proved to be very coherent, and they significantly complement Elias's other writings on civilising processes, state formation and social conflicts in early modern Europe, and on established-outsiders relations. The design for the studies of the genesis of the naval profession was broader than for merely the three articles announced as intended for the *British Journal of Sociology*. In the archive an outline was found with a plan for a publication comprising *seven* chapters, as follows:

1   Gentlemen into seamen
2   Some data on the genesis of the English navy
3   Collaboration and dissensions between soldiers and sailors
    (a) The relationship between master and lieutenant
    (b) The professional feud between gentleman-commanders and tarpaulin commanders
4   The social origin of the naval officers of the seventeenth century
5   The growth of the naval hierarchy and the development of the naval career[2]
6   The development of the naval profession in France. Differences between the French and the English naval profession and their causes
7   General survey of the state of the naval profession during the eighteenth and the beginning of the nineteenth century.[3]

Elias had clearly intended to publish a book on the topic, and in particular a chapter on maritime supremacy comparing developments in England with those in Spain and France seems to form an integral part of the intended design of the book. The outline served as our guide in compiling and reconstructing the naval studies. From abundant material and a multitude of different versions in the archive, we have tried to put together a book that comes as close to Elias's original intentions as possible.

Elias's enquiry deals with the social origins of one of the key institutions in British society, the navy and its officer corps. In general the work is built on the strife between two strata in English society, on the one hand the gentlemen – members of the nobility and the landed gentry – and on the other the merchants and artisans. The rivalry between these two groups contributed to the institutionalisation of a new occupation, that of the naval officer. Effective command in the navy required both nautical skills and military competence. Military skills stemmed from the values and habitus of noblemen (courage, fighting spirit, collaboration, discipline, hierarchical command structures).[4] Nautical skills originated among seamen or 'tarpaulin commanders' who had learned the tricks of the trade as young apprentices to the sea. Though often the subject of dispute, the need for officers to acquire nautical skills became more and more evident. But the gentlemen resented being forced to do what they regarded as the lowly work of the seamen, whose manual labour, an inherent part of a mariner's job, was deemed dishonourable for gentlemen. Elias therefore formulated the following key question: *How could a gentleman become a tarpaulin without losing caste, without lowering his social status?*[5]

His thesis was that only the rivalry between the two socially divergent groups could result in a fusion of military and nautical skills, or, in other words, the sociogenesis of the naval officer. The rivalry was essential both for England's gaining a competitive edge and for its dominance of the world's seas. In Spain and in France, these rivalries and conflicts were subdued, with detrimental results to both nautical skills and military competence.

But how did Elias come to choose to focus on this question?

3

ELIAS AND THE PROFESSIONS

For Elias personally, the studies on the naval profession can be seen as part of his drive to understand and orientate himself to his country of adoption. Three years after the publication of the article in the *BJS*, Elias took British citizenship. His extensive reading in British history and culture is evident in many later publications, notably in the essays of the 1960s and 1970s on the sociology of sport (which culminated in the publication with Eric Dunning of *Quest for Excitement*) but also in many three-way comparisons that he drew between Britain, France and Germany, for instance in *The Germans*.[6]

The naval research was undertaken for the Social Research Division of the London School of Economics, and Elias thanked H. L. Beales of the LSE for his encouragement (p. 134 below). It seems likely that the research was begun when Elias was appointed a Senior Research Fellow at the LSE just after the publication of *Über den Prozeß der Zivilisation* in 1939 – or at least grew out of the work that he was doing during that period. The choice of topic probably also seemed a good one to Elias not only from the point of view of personal interest, but also for his prospects of securing a career in a British university. The professions, in a quite specific sense, were widely discussed by British sociologists as a key feature of British society, from the publication in 1933 of Carr-Saunders and Wilson's book *The Professions* (to which Elias refers, p. 135 below) until about the mid-1970s.[7] Elias's research can thus be seen as a means of adapting not just to British society but also to British sociology.

The professions – especially the law and medicine – had attracted the attention of leading sociologists in the English-speaking world on both sides of the Atlantic. Talcott Parsons (1902–79), who from the 1940s to the 1960s was the world's most prominent sociological theorist, had in an early essay asked why in the modern economy the membership of professional as well as business occupations had grown so markedly.[8] But in Britain the peculiar significance of 'the professions' was that the term had long been used to denote a relatively small number of occupations that it was respectable for a *gentleman* to pursue. These occupations were, moreover, perceived to be an important part of the British national power structure. Over the centuries, the range of occupations qualifying to be counted as 'professions' in this sense changed and expanded (as indeed did the definition of a 'gentleman'). Nevertheless, there were continuities. The main points of sociological interest in the professions were later summed up by Elias himself in a succinct dictionary entry.[9] The term 'profession', he wrote, denotes occupations that demanded 'highly specialised knowledge and skill acquired at least in part by courses of a more or less theoretical nature and not by practice alone, tested by some form of examination either at university or some other authorised institution, and conveying to the persons who possess them considerable authority in relation to "clients"'. That authority was maintained and enhanced by self-regulating professional associations, which laid down rules of entry to the profession, standards of knowledge, and remuneration. A 'profession' was an occupation whose members gave a service rather than produced goods or sold them for profit,[10] and it did not involve manual work – with some exceptions, such as surgeons, where the manual skill is related to knowledge acquired through academic and scientific training. Originally, the term applied to the clergy, lawyers and physicians – occupations in which a gentleman, such as a younger son of a landowning family that lived off rents and other forms of unearned income, could make a living without engaging in manual work. The scope of the word gradually widened over the centuries. University dons, most of whom were until the nineteenth century clerics themselves, and army and navy officers were among the first groups admitted to the growing ranks of what were recognised as professions, followed by civil servants, architects and others.[11] Then, in the course of the twentieth century, in a broader sense the word came to apply to all occupations requiring some academic training or scientific knowledge in the form of degrees or diplomas, qualifications that by the beginning of the twenty-first century were in many Western countries awarded to more than half of the cohort of young people.

Two of the last prominent discussions of the professions in the original sense are to be found in the work of a younger colleague of Elias at Leicester: in 1972 Terence Johnson summarised several decades of research and discussion in his book *Professions and Power*; and the following year he contributed a chapter to an introductory textbook of sociology that emanated from the Leicester department.[12] From then onwards, the topic seemed to become less central to the interests of British sociologists. One reason was undoubtedly that in the 1960s and 1970s, in Britain as in many other countries, long-standing patterns of authority came under challenge, and old hierarchies were weakened. A much wider range of occupations was now open to people from relatively well-off strata, while admission to the formerly exclusive professions was gained by more people from lower strata. These trends were reflected in a quite sudden and dramatic widening of the use of the word 'profession': the 'professional' footballer and his 'professional foul' had arrived. Of wider consequence, at the end of the millennium it had become common for press and politicians to question the basis of the old professions, by casting doubt on whether civil servants, lawyers and doctors were really acting in the public interest, and indeed asking whether self-regulation permitted conspiracy *against* the public interest.[13]

'The professions' in the traditional sense remained a staple of the undergraduate curriculum for about four decades. Yet if Elias imagined he was addressing a topic of central interest among British sociologists, and that his article in the *BJS* would attract interest in his ideas and help him to gain a secure university post, he was sorely disappointed.

6

A DIFFICULT RECEPTION

Why did the article on the naval profession in the 1950 *BJS* arouse so little interest? The principal answer is that British sociologists – even though a then small circle, most of whose members knew each other personally – were unfamiliar with Elias's earlier work, and he could not possibly have appeared to them then as the substantial intellectual figure that we now recognise. For a man who was already 53 years of age when the *BJS* article was published, Elias had published remarkably few items, and almost all in German.[14] *Über den Prozeß der Zivilisation*, now recognised as Elias's masterpiece, had been published obscurely in Basel in 1939, but was little known even to those who could read German, and it was not published in English translation until 1978–82. Indeed Elias, for whatever reason, seems to have been unhelpful towards earlier efforts to secure its translation into English.[15] A short version of another major work, eventually to appear as *The Court Society*, had been written as Elias's dissertation for his *Habilitation* at Frankfurt in 1933, immediately before he fled into exile; but it was not completed in its now familiar form until the late 1960s.[16] The research with his Leicester student John Scotson, which eventuated in *The Established and the Outsiders*, was not begun until the late 1950s.[17] All his other books and most of his essays were published in his years of retirement.

The scantiness of Elias's published output in the late 1940s and 1950s must be related to this being a most difficult period in his life. After surviving for four years (1935–9) on a meagre stipend from a charity for Jewish refugees, Elias gained employment as a Senior Research Fellow at the London School of Economics, but his work for the LSE was interrupted by internment as an enemy alien in 1940. Then, in 1942, came the death of his mother in Auschwitz, which Elias always afterwards regarded as the great trauma of his life. After the war Elias had no secure employment, and made a precarious living by teaching extra-mural classes. With his friend Siegmund

7

Foulkes, he helped lay the theoretical foundations of the important Group Analysis form of psychotherapy, and he also went into psychoanalysis himself. When asked why, he said the most immediate reason was that he wrote so slowly: 'I was unhappy that I did not produce more, although I had so many ideas'.[18] But he also wrote to Cas Wouters that the analysis helped him get beyond 'an ineradicable guilt feeling that I was unable to get my mother out of the concentration camp before she died in a gas chamber'.[19] This difficult period continued until 1954 when, at the age of 57, Elias finally secured a permanent position in the academic world, at the then University College Leicester.

In short, when he was working on the studies of the naval profession, Elias was experiencing hard times. He could only have been more discouraged by the negligible impact of the 1950 *BJS* article, intended to be the first of three. One of the reasons why the other studies were not published may well have been that the first one did not provoke any response.

Goudsblom tracked references to the article by later sociologists.[20] He found only three, in the work of Lammers and of Teitler.[21] He overlooked a small but interesting reference in Morris Janowitz's classic *The Professional Soldier*; in the context of his own discussion of the social background of military officers, Janowitz cited Elias's essay in support of these remarks:

> Most fundamentally, the professional soldier is conservative, since his social origin is grounded in the history of the post-feudal nobility in Europe and its social equivalents in the United States. … Interestingly, in the origins of the naval profession, as represented by the British Navy, there was greater reliance on middle- and even lower-class personnel in the officer corps, because men were needed to perform the arduous and skilled tasks of managing a vessel and its crew.[22]

These references belong to the field of military sociology. But even in military sociology Elias's work has not been much used, and the 'studies in the genesis of the naval profession' are not mentioned in recent reviews and studies on the military profession.[23]

For purposes of comparison with Elias's work, Teitler's 1974 thesis is the most interesting. It was translated and published in 1977 by the most important institution in military sociology, the Inter-University Seminar on Armed Forces and Society. Significantly, the book was called *The Genesis of the Professional Officers' Corps*.

Teitler had studied sociology at the University of Amsterdam. Jacques van Doorn, one of the most renowned military sociologists of the time, was Teitler's doctoral supervisor.[24] Van Doorn collaborated with Janowitz and Lammers on many occasions, and – in a dispute about the merits of American functionalist sociology as compared with figurational sociology that is relevant to the theoretical context of the naval profession studies – crossed swords with Elias's most prominent Dutch advocate Johan Goudsblom.[25] As the work of Elias first became popular in Amsterdam, these biographical facts concerning Teitler explain why he was aware of works like *The Civilising Process*, *The Court Society* and the 1950 *BJS* article. Teitler did not know Elias's unpublished work, but the similarities between the two authors are striking. Teitler elaborates the history and the sociogenesis of the naval profession, and arrives, more or less, at the same conclusion as Elias: the professionalisation of the military occupation was first completed in England because of the openness of social strata, and because of the amalgamation of military and civilian skills through the creative aspects of non-subdued conflicts between the different social groups. That argument is very much in line with *The Civilising Process*. But there are also many differences between the two scholars. The line of reasoning, sources of evidence and analysis differ completely.[26] One of the differences is that Teitler delves more deeply into the role of battle technique, technology and tactics. The manner of fighting is more central to his argument, whereas Elias concentrates on the conflicts between people on board ship. As evidence, Teitler uses Dutch maritime history and contrasts it with France and England. Elias mentions the Dutch case only twice, to point his readers to the exceptional character of Dutch maritime development.

When Elias gained recognition in the 1970s, a translation of the study 'Drake and Doughty' was published in the prominent Dutch intellectual magazine *De Gids*.[27] Though the story is wonderful, it made little sense publishing it out of its context. As will become evident in this book, the powerful meaning of the story vanishes without its wider context, for it depends on the totality of the argument. In fact, this was also the weak point of the first study published in *BJS*, but – besides the obvious fact that the potential readership for a publication in Dutch is much smaller than in English – the effect of isolation proved to be more detrimental to this second piece. When read in context, the story stands out as an illustration strengthening the central argument – one of the jewels in the crown, sparkling and shining brightly. As an article standing alone it is merely an anecdotal story about a conflict between two long dead privateers.

Such impact as the *BJS* article did have came partly indirectly, through his colleagues and students at Leicester. Elias's ideas in the article on 'gentlemen and tarpaulins' influenced the chapter on 'the professions' in the 1973 textbook edited by Geoffrey Hurd; and Christopher Dandeker, one of the students from the Leicester period, who also published on the naval officers' profession in the *BJS*, introduced Eliasian ideas into military sociology.[28]

In 1998 Goudsblom and Mennell published a small part of the *BJS* article in *The Norbert Elias Reader*, a book that is intended as a 'biographical selection'.[29] Recently, two translations of the *BJS* article have been published in French, in the military sociology journal *Les Champs de Mars*, and in Portuguese.[30]

Elias must have been disappointed by the *BJS* article being received with such indifference in sociological circles. He clearly postponed publication of the other studies. But Elias never entirely abandoned the project. In 1983 he presented the study of the naval profession to a French-German audience in Paris, where he spoke in German. He said: 'das was ich zu sagen habe, ist ein Ausschnitt aus einem Project, das wie ich glaube, jedenfalls in meiner Lebenszeit nicht mehr zustande kommen wird.' [What I have to say, is part of a project, which, I believe, will not be finished during my lifetime]. He also apologised that 'ich veröffentliche sehr langsam' [I publish very slowly]. After these words he gave a résumé of the project.[31] Elias knew that his time was running out, but the apology that he was so slow in publishing and the remark that 'the project will not be finished during my lifetime' appear to indicate that he would have liked to see the project published.

THE SOCIOLOGICAL SIGNIFICANCE OF 'THE GENESIS OF THE NAVAL PROFESSION'

Goudsblom observed that 'Readers familiar with [Elias's] other work would have recognised easily the general sociological significance of this paper', but he added that, since most readers in 1950 were not familiar with it, they would have thought that the article was an 'historical contribution of limited importance'.[32] Equally, from an historian's point of view, Elias probably appeared to be painting with too broad a brush, writing in general terms about a long-term process of development rather than concentrating on the age of Pepys when the controversy between gentlemen and tarpaulins was at its height. The difference is apparent when *The Genesis of the Naval Profession* is compared with just such an historical study, J. D. Davies's *Gentlemen and Tarpaulins*, published four decades after the *BJS* article.[33] Davies's study concentrates on a much shorter period of time, from the Restoration of Charles II in 1660 until the deposition of his brother James II in the Glorious Revolution of 1688. Within that period, he uses all the original sources on which Elias drew and many more besides, as well as having the benefit of the secondary sources produced through 40 more years of research in naval history. He mentioned the 1950 *BJS* article in his bibliography, but appeared to make no further use of it. Davies produced a first-class, absorbing account of the politics of the navy at that time, in far greater depth than Elias attempted. On the other hand, he showed little interest in the broader sociological questions about the formation of a profession, still less about the longer-term processes of social development that preoccupied Elias; as Elias noted in an essay he wrote in the late 1960s, among historians there is a widespread tendency to perceive unstructured 'change', but not long-term structured processes of social development.[34] Davies noted that, during these two reigns, the conflict between gentlemen and tarpaulins became somewhat more muted and the distinction somewhat less sharp, as the gentlemen acquired more nautical knowledge. But Davies did not pursue the question that can now be seen – especially in the light of the hitherto unpublished parts of Elias's study – to have been central to Elias's project: why did this happen in England and not elsewhere, and what were the consequences for maritime power?

'Comparative sociology', remarked Émile Durkheim, 'is not a particular branch of sociology; it is sociology itself, in so far as it ceases to be purely descriptive and aspires to account for facts.'[35] In this respect, if in no other, Elias was a follower of Durkheim. Spain and France, Elias pointed out, faced the same problem as England: their officers lacked nautical skills and their seamen were not trained to be military leaders. However, the barrier between gentlemen officers and craftsmen officers on board ship was higher and more rigid in France than in England, and higher in Spain than in France. In both countries, the process of integration and differentiation that in England led to the formation of a single officer corps, ran into obstacles.

Spain, in the late medieval period up to 1500, is described by Elias as a racist society. The presence of a different racial group, the Moors, served to influence developments in Spain negatively. None of the 'whites' – probably the earliest use of that now familiar term – was willing to do manual labour. This helped to prevent Spain from becoming a manufacturing country, a great commercial power, and a great sea power.

In France, the powerful central bureaucracy could order changes from above, much more easily than could the English Admiralty. Colbert's reform made the French navy, for a time in the late seventeenth century, a formidable threat to its competitors. In the end, however, the French navy proved inferior to the English naval forces. Bureaucracy was one of the reasons for the 'inferiority' of the French naval forces because it caused the French officers to be overcautious. Whenever an action went wrong, officers had to give a full account of events for which they were held fully responsible. This caused them to avoid risk-taking, and to resort to fighting using guns only. The French preferred not to fight using the old boarding techniques and kept their distance, forcing the English to do the same. The English preferred to rely on their nautical skill, for they tended to be more skilful sailors than the French. Another, no less important factor in the decline of the French navy and its inferiority most of the time to the naval force of England was the social distance between sailors and commanding nobles that was reinforced by Louis XIV's constitution for his naval forces. This constitution assured supreme control for the nobles.

Although Elias scarcely refers to it, the position of the other rival power at sea, the Dutch United Provinces, was very different.[36] Compared with England, the rivalry in the navy between nobility and seamen was much milder. The nobility, as in many other continental countries, was more oriented towards the army, causing the sailors to be the dominant group on board. Furthermore, merchant interests prevailed over military interests. The Dutch Navy, lagging behind in gunnery technology and the development of bigger ships, specialised in the older techniques of boarding and, in these techniques, they became at least as skilled as the English. In conflicts

13

with the Dutch, the English gained the upper hand not because of nautical skills, but because of military skills such as the use of their superior firepower. To deploy the firepower of the guns to the full, the English had to fight in line, avoiding the old techniques of boarding.[37] So this led to the situation that, in conflicts with the French, nautical skills were most important to the English, whereas military skills had to prevail in their conflicts with the Dutch.

England's political system proved to be a most successful stimulus for the development of the navy. Its navy acquired an unchallenged position of dominance on the seas.[38] In the end, England's supremacy was due both to this political structure and to the rivalries between rising commoners and the nobility trying to hold on to old privileges.

> Although the initial antagonism between the two groups was essentially a social and professional antagonism, it was in its ups and downs and finally in its outcome closely connected with the great struggle between court nobility and middle class England and more especially, between their social standard. . . . On the continent (with exception of the Netherlands) there was a matching rivalry between nobility and civilians but separation in naval forces. Continental forces copied the more successful British pattern (but with difficulty because social structures resisted and had to be changed).[39]

The need for change was apparent and stemmed from international competition. Elias concludes: 'England had to become a great maritime power or else, as an island nation, she would have suffered a fate worse than that of Spain'.[40] Figure 1 summarises the developments in the four maritime countries. On the one hand societies have to permit a certain degree of openness as a precondition for the amalgamation of two groups of people, and on the other hand the fusion of groups which is the answer to processes of specialisation and integration can only be brought about when conflicts are played out in the open. Rivalries must not be stifled.

14

Figure 1: *Conditions of society favourable to the rise of England as a maritime power*

Amalgamation/openness of classes

	Yes	No
Yes	Holland (regents dominant)	England
No	Spain France	

Yes   No

Rivalries subdued

Military skills

	−	+
+	Spain France	Fusion in England
−		Holland

−   +

Civilian skills

The triangular comparison that Elias makes between the naval regimes of England France and Spain clearly arose out of his earlier attempt to explain the rise of absolutist monarchies in early modern Europe. Particularly central to his argument in *The Genesis of the Naval Profession* is his concept of 'the royal mechanism', which he had developed at length in *The Civilising Process*; its relevance was also seized upon by Teitler in his own work on the naval profession.[41] Like any other individual person in the face of pressure from a whole network of interdependent people, a king would have little power if his whole society, or a considerable part of it, stood together against him. But, reasoned Elias

> the hour of the strong central authority within a highly differentiated society strikes when the ambivalence of interests of the most important functional groups grows so large, and power is distributed so evenly between them, that there can be neither a decisive compromise nor a decisive conflict between them.

The reason why, in such a figuration, the major social groups – the nobility, gentry, merchants, artisans and their various divisions – do not make common cause against the monarchy is that 'they tie each

other's hands'.[42] They do that because, with the advancing division
of social functions, human relationships acquire a special quality of
'open or latent *ambivalence*'. It is when these circumstances arise
that the 'royal mechanism' functions effectively. Elias illuminates
the principle by comparing it to a tug-of-war between two very
evenly balanced sides. Both sides heave with all their might, but
neither can dislodge the other from its position. Great forces are at
work, but they are locked up in the tremendous tension in the rope.
In this situation, a single person who is able to interpose his own
strength first on one side, then on the other, can control the whole
contest. He need not be very strong in himself: probably he could
not withstand the pull of one of the sides alone, certainly not both
pulling together. Yet the forces arranged as they are form a 'machine'
which magnifies the effect of his smallest effort. On the other hand
he has to take great care not to allow the tension itself to be relaxed,
nor permit either side to gain a clear advantage; real tugs-of-war
usually end up in collapse. Kings therefore tended to favour whatever group was in the secondary power position in order to mani-
pulate the power balances in the kingdom.[43] In the case of the English
navy, the King's commissioning policy became a tool for this purpose.
In Henry VIII's time, the old nobility was already on the decline but
was still the most powerful group. To counterbalance the influence
of the old nobility the King frequently appointed men from inferior
status as commanders. During the reign of Charles I, the balance of
forces in the country had changed and the urban bourgeoisie was
definitely on the rise. The King therefore favoured courtiers in
awarding commissions. He lacked political skill in maintaining the
delicate balance of tensions in his favour, however, and in pursuing
the creation in England of an absolutist monarchy on the continental
model, he provoked a civil war; as one small part of his overall
strategy, his commissioning policy helped to ensure that the navy
took the side of parliament. After the Restoration, as Davies shows,
his sons had to be much more even-handed in their treatment of

gentleman and tarpaulin officers; this was in accordance with a shift in the central balances of power in English society, as, from the mid seventeenth century to the early eighteenth, it underwent a cycle of violence, the outcome of which Elias discussed in more detail in a later essay.[44] In contrast, the more effective absolutist monarchy in France continued to privilege the aristocracy in the award of commissions, but to the detriment of the effectiveness of its navy. That was only one small part of a more general stultifying of the royal mechanism that contributed in the end to the outbreak of the French Revolution.[45]

Another key concept of Elias's that plays a key part in *The Genesis of the Naval Profession* is that of 'established–outsiders' relationships. The point is obscured by the fact that he did not use that precise term until the mid-1960s.[46] But the idea itself is clearly expressed when Elias writes (pp. 49–50 below):

> one can say that similar status-battles and struggles for position, longer or shorter as the case may be, can be found whenever individuals, initially independent, are about to merge into a group, or smaller groups into a larger. In that sense, the tensions and conflicts between soldiers and mariners, between gentlemen and seamen in the history of the naval profession, may serve as a simple model for other more complex conflicts and struggles in the history of mankind.

Here, it is clear that Elias is thinking especially of his earlier discussion of the formation of a new upper class, in Renaissance Europe, from elements of diverse social background.[47] That process, he argued, had been a driving force in the formalisation and elaboration of codes of manners, one of the hallmarks of the European civilising process. In the case of the navy, a similar process arising from the conflict between gentlemen and tarpaulins eventuated in a new institutional pattern, the rank of midshipman, and a new kind of officer corps.

In *The Genesis of the Naval Profession* Elias did not, however, use just particular concepts from his earlier work in isolation; this book, albeit early and unfinished, is a clear example of Elias's overall conception of sociology, which came much later to be known as 'figurational' or 'process' sociology.

In his published writings, for the most part Elias talks much less about 'methods of research' than does the typical sociologist, and he disliked the word 'methodology' for its philosophical connotations. Nevertheless, he did have a method, even if it is often left implicit. In fact there are over 100 pages of 'scrap notes' in the folders for the work on the naval profession in the Elias archive that are dedicated to methods – a sure indication that the naval study was not just a pastime but a major project. Some notes and remarks are in German. One note bears the title 'Die Eliassche Methode' and contains the key phrase 'Makrostrukturen durch die Untersuchung von Mikrostructuren sichtbar zu machen' [to reveal macro structures by researching micro structures].[48] Another observation is that 'The history of a profession is part of the social and economic history of its country'.[49]

These notes show that the main object of the project on the naval profession was more far-reaching than Elias's key question – 'How could a gentleman become a tarpaulin without losing caste, without lowering his social status?' – suggests. The studies are in fact investigations into England's culture, national and international politics, social structure and economy.[50] By studying the roots of a part of English culture – namely the genesis of a profession – Elias is trying to gain an insight in the specific civilising processes that made Britain into an empire.

The study of social processes and the emergence of new forms of social institution through unfolding social conflicts – what Elias called sociogenesis – is linked to the study of psychogenesis, or the changes in personality structures or habitus (the socially learned 'second nature' that individuals acquire in the process of socialisation). It is the study of the network of interactions that distinguishes

figurational studies from systems approaches and individual psychological perspectives.[51]

Conflict is central to Elias's sociological thinking. As he wrote, 'if
one attempted to work out a general theory of institutions one would
probably have to say that the initial conflict is one of the basic
features of a nascent institution' (p. 49). The studies in the genesis of
the naval profession sharpen our perception of his contribution to
the sociological understanding of conflict. An illustrative contrast
can be drawn between Elias's naval studies and George Homans's
far more famous essay on 'The small warship' published four years
earlier.[52] Homans, drawing on his own experience in the US navy
during the Second World War, discussed a ship's crew much as if it
were any other workgroup, and was concerned with questions about
effective leadership and the maintenance of morale, in the style of
the 'human relations' school of industrial management; there was
none of Elias's awareness of the ties of interdependence between the
relationships among a ship's crew far out at sea and the history,
broader social conflicts and shifting power structure of the home
society. Elias attacked the 'consensus' sociology of Durkheim. In the
archives, the texts from which we have derived chapter 3 are pre-
ceded by an introduction by Elias that debunks Durkheim's sociology.
Apparently Elias wanted to stress the difference between his approach
and Durkheim's theory of the division of labour. Elias wrote:

> Durkheim could still affirm his belief that the division of labour
> normally produces solidarity. And although later on he apparently had
> some doubts in view of the recurrent conflicts of an industrial society,
> he still maintained that solidarity was the normal result of division of
> labour and strife an abnormality.
>
> Today the problem confronting Durkheim, in theory and prac-
> tice, is as acute as it was in his time. Increasing specialisation seems to
> produce both specific forms of solidarity and co-operation and specific
> forms of tensions and conflict. Both specific forms of solidarity and

co-operation as well as forms of tensions and conflicts seem to follow from increasing specialisation. But in the light of our slowly expanding knowledge of facts, one can see more clearly the connection between these seemingly contradictory effects, and can re-state his problem in a different form.

Increasing specialisation, one may say, results in increasing interdependence of more and more people. After a time, often after a long time, increased dependence on each other may induce people to evolve closer ties that may lead to willing and ordered institutional forms of ordered co-operation and strong feelings of solidarity.

But ordered and willing co-operation and a feeling of solidarity do not follow, as it were, automatically from an increase in interdependence. At best they are the outcome of a long process of adjustment to changing conditions; and this adjustment may take a very long time.[53]

He thus criticised Durkheim's assumption that increasing interdependence would lead to solidarity. Elias proposes a conflict-centred form of sociology as a better way to understand social change. The manner in which this sociology of tensions is constructed resembles Marx's dialectical method.[54] In particular, the concept of an 'axis of tensions' is an example of this dialectical approach. From tensions between nobility and bourgeoisie in the seventeenth century to the eighteenth and nineteenth centuries, 'the main axis of tensions, shifted more definitely to the commercial and industrial section of the population, dividing it into two camps, the working classes and the middle classes' (p. 40 below). Remarking that the history of a profession is part of the social and economic history of a country, Elias – in these studies – proves to be very close to a Marxist perspective. In his Paris lecture in 1983 Elias himself pointed to the resemblance with Marx, but he also viewed the Marxist schema as too crude.

Das Marxsche Schema . . . ist gewiss nicht falsch, aber es ist grob! . . . Was bei der Marxschen Klassenteilung fehlt, ist die Tatsache, dass der

König und der Adel einen Machtbrennpunkt eigener Art darstellte, der nicht schlechterdings mit dem Adel gleichzusetzen ist.

[The Marxist model . . . is certainly not wrong, but it is crude! . . . What is missing in the Marxist divide of classes is the fact that the king and the nobles form a kind of focus of power in their own particular way, that is not equal to the nobility.][55]

In the Paris lecture, Elias criticised Marx's two-party dialectics and presented the royal mechanism as at least a three-party kind of dialectics. So the studies on the naval profession can be seen – apparently with Elias's permission – as a sophisticated version of Marxist conflict sociology.

LATER RESEARCH ON THE NAVAL PROFESSION

No doubt some details of what Elias wrote may need revision in the light of subsequent historical research. N. A. M. Rodger's magisterial *The Safeguard of the Sea* and *The Command of the Ocean*[56] synthesise a vast body of evidence. They contain much information on the social background of naval commanders. Rodger tends to emphasise how many gentlemen (for instance Lord Howard of Effingham in Drake's time) taught themselves the essential nautical skills. He concludes that the gap between 'gentlemen' and 'tarpaulins' was exaggerated in the Restoration period, when tensions aboard ship had already in general been muted. Nevertheless, the *rhetoric* of 'gentlemen and tarpaulins' in that period corresponded to persisting political and social tensions ashore. Davies's *Gentlemen and Tarpaulins*, if understood as a test of Elias's thesis, misfires because to examine the working of the royal mechanism would require a study at least from the reign of Henry VIII to the time of William and Mary.

Padfield's account of Britain's rise to maritime supremacy is partly compatible with Elias's.[57] Padfield points to the positive sides of open social systems (and hence the creative side of moderate rivalry and competition) as a stimulus for professional seamanship leading to naval superiority, and to the paralysing effects of bureaucracy in France. According to Padfield, military supremacy on land (France under Napoleon, Germany under Hitler, Russia under Stalin) seems correlated with authoritarian political regimes, which will fail in the end. But in Padfield's work it is not clear whether it is open democratic systems that further maritime supremacy, or whether it is maritime supremacy that furthers democracy. Of course, it is possible that both are true, but if Padfield is advancing a process theory in the style of Elias, it is one that lacks Elias's explanatory clarity.

CONCLUSIONS

In contrast to most postmodern sociology or the sociology of globalisation, where the military factor is played down or neglected, Elias is sensitive to the role of war and the military in the formation of empires. Tilly formulated the correlation between state formation and the military factor very well when he remarked: 'War made the state and the state made war'.[58] Change, civilising processes and empire building are, in Elias's work, closely connected to the study of the military. The studies in the genesis of the naval profession are excellent examples of military sociology. But they are more than military sociology or sociology of the professions. Elias aimed at a higher goal. They are about civilisation, empire building and changing standards of behaviour all at the same time.

Returning to the question of why his studies on the genesis of the naval profession were never properly published, the answer now seems obvious. In the 1950s Elias's earlier work was not well known. When he proposed a series of articles to the *BJS*, the readers were unable to see its importance and its connection to the larger theoretical framework developed in *The Civilising Process*. The translation of 'Drake and Doughty' and its publication in *De Gids* also proved to be an unsuccessful publication strategy. When published in isolation, the wider meaning of this intriguing story vanishes. Had it been published as originally intended, as the second part of three studies, the story of the conflict between Drake and Doughty would have built up the suspense. The relevance of the studies on the naval profession would have been more easily recognisable if they had been published as a whole, preferably in book format; and it is precisely for this reason that we have compiled this book from the fragments that were preserved in the archives. Now that the studies are published in this volume, we hope that they will be recognised as a seminal study not only on the genesis of a profession but also as a study of the naval and maritime roots of England's culture and England's empire.

EDITORIAL POLICY

In preparing the text of *The Genesis of the Naval Profession*, we have inevitably had to allow ourselves more latitude in editorial judgement than is possible for the editors of the volumes of the Collected Works of Norbert Elias. They are dealing with texts that Elias authorised for publication, while we have been handling for the most part unfinished drafts. We have throughout given details of which folders in the Norbert Elias papers we have drawn upon, so that anyone who goes to Marbach may easily trace what we have included and what we have omitted. For the rest, we have largely followed the practice that has been decided upon by the editorial advisory committee for the Collected Works when the source texts were written by Elias in English. When he wrote in English, he only occasionally made minor grammatical mistakes, but it is often evident that his word order and punctuation are strongly influenced by his native German. So, in the published 1950 *BJS* article as well as in the unpublished typescripts, besides correcting typographical and minor grammatical errors, small changes have been made silently to punctuation and word order, provided that such changes in no way alter the sense of the text. In a handful of cases where the changes were more substantial, Elias's original wording is given in the Textual Variants. We have also occasionally inserted extra words, in square brackets, for clarification of the meaning.

Like most writers in the 1950s, Elias unselfconsciously used what would later be called 'gender-specific vocabulary' – that is, he often wrote 'men' when he meant 'human beings' or 'people'. Later, again like most writers, he came to feel this was wrong and, with his authority, in books and essays brought to publication later in his life, 'men' was generally changed to 'people'. This is not a major problem in *The Genesis of the Naval Profession* because here he is writing about an almost entirely masculine world, but there are one or two instances where we have made the necessary adjustment.

Apart from the title for chapter 1, which is that of the 1950 *BJS* article, the chapter titles have been supplied by the editors. So have all the subheadings within chapters, including those in chapter 1. Notes added by the editors, and additions by the editors to Elias's notes, are indicated by '– eds'. We have had some difficulty in tracking down works that Elias cited inaccurately, but in most cases we have succeeded. In the typescripts from which we have drawn chapter 2, there are also some reference numbers indicating where Elias intended there be a footnote, but the notes themselves are missing. In a few cases we were able to work out to what they were meant to refer. Where we were unable to do so, and where the citation is for a direct quotation, we have indicated that the note is missing, but otherwise we have simply eliminated the reference numbers.

The Genesis of the Naval Profession

I

Gentlemen and Tarpaulins

INTRODUCTION: ON PROFESSIONS

Professions, stripped of their gear and apparel,[1] are specialised social functions which people perform in response to specialised needs of others; they are, at least in their fully developed form, institutionalised sets of human relationships. The study of the genesis of a profession, therefore, is not simply a study of a number of individuals who first performed certain functions for others and entered into certain relationships with others, but that of these functions and relationships themselves.

They all, professions, occupations or whatever their name may be, are in a peculiar way independent, not of people, but of those particular people by whom they are represented at a given time. They continue to exist when their present representatives die. Like languages, they presuppose the existence of a whole group. And if they change, if new occupations emerge within a community, again, these changes are not simply due to acts or thoughts of this or that particular person, not even to those of a scientist or an inventor. It is the changing situation of a whole community which creates the conditions for the rise of a new occupation and determines its course of development.

Scientific discoveries and inventions, new specialised means for the satisfaction of human needs, are undoubtedly factors in the development of a new occupation; so are new human needs themselves.

But neither of these two factors is by itself its fountainhead and its source. They depend on each other for their development. Human needs become differentiated and specific only in conjunction with specialised human techniques;[2] these on their part emerge and crystallise into occupations only in view of potential or actual human needs.[3] The rise of a new occupation, therefore, is not due to the rise of new needs or the rise of new techniques alone, but to the interplay between both. It is, in essence, a process of trial and error[4] in which people attempt to match occupational techniques or institutions and human needs. Every single step in this direction is executed by individuals. Yet, the process as such, the genesis and development of a profession, or of any other occupation, is more than the sum total of individual acts. It has a pattern of its own.

For specific maladjustments, discrepancies of one kind or another between professional institutions and the needs they serve, and tensions between groups of people engendered by these discrepancies, impose their pattern upon individuals. They, not individuals as such, are the main levers of a profession's development. The adjustment of institutions and needs, in steadily changing societies, is never complete. Discrepancies may arise at one time more from changes in technique, at another more from changes in social conditions and requirements. Whatever their immediate cause, they create specific difficulties; they produce frictions and conflicts; they confront every member of a profession with problems not of their own making. However, as soon as they enter a profession, these institutional problems become their own problems, these difficulties their own difficulties, these conflicts their own conflicts. Nor are the solutions entirely in their own hands. Sometimes changing social conditions favour adjustment; at others, they delay it or block it altogether. It may happen, as it happened in fact early in the history of the naval profession, that, for several generations, people become involved time after time in professional conflicts of the same type, wrestle again and again with the same professional problems, and, knowing what seems an ideal solution, are unable to bring it about. In all these cases, the problems are set for the individual by the web of social functions into which he enters, with its inherent disparities between means and ends. Impelled by them, he continues with his short-term aims what he did not start, the long-term development of his profession.

In historical studies, the development of professions and other institutions often appears as a smooth and steady progress towards 'perfection' – the 'perfection' of our time. Attention is frequently focused more on the institutional façade, as it appears in this period and then in the next and finally in the present, and less on the actual human relationships behind the façade. Yet it is only by visualising these institutions as part of a wide network of human relationships, by resurrecting for our own understanding the recurrent difficulties and conflicts with which people in the orbit of these institutions struggled within this network, that one can comprehend why and how the institutional framework itself emerged and changed from period to period. The unsolved problems raised in the minds of contemporaries by the shortcomings of their professional institutions are, in other words, as essential a part of the history of these institutions as the solution itself. In retrospect, the solution comes to life only when seen together with the formerly unsolved problems. If one comes face to face, behind the more impersonal façade, with people struggling, often in vain, to adjust their inherited institutional framework with all its incongruities to what they feel to be their own needs, then the atmosphere so often surrounding old institutions in history books - the atmosphere of museum pieces - evaporates.[a] In that respect, the people of the past are on a par with us; or rather we with them.

'THE SEAMEN WERE NOT GENTLEMEN; AND THE GENTLEMEN WERE NOT SEAMEN'[5]

The naval profession grew into shape at a time when the navy was a fleet of sailing ships. In many respects, therefore, the training, duties and standards of naval officers were different from those of our time. It has been said that the command of a modern ship with its elaborate technical equipment requires a scientifically trained mind. That of a sailing ship required the mind of a craftsman. Only people apprenticed to the sea early in life could hope to master it. 'To catch 'em young' was a well-known slogan of the old navy. It was quite normal for a young boy to start on his future career as naval officer at the age of nine or ten directly on board ship. Many experienced people thought it almost too late if he came on board at the age of fourteen, not only because he had to find his 'sea-legs', and to overcome seasickness as early as possible, but because the art of splicing and knotting, the general rudiments of rigging, the proper way of going aloft – grasping the shroud and not the ratlines – and a host of other more complicated operations could be learned only by long and hard practice. To acquire understanding of sailing ships people had to work, at least for a time, with their hands. Book learning was of little avail.

At the same time, all naval officers, at least from the eighteenth century on, regarded themselves, and wished to be regarded by others, as gentlemen. To master the mariner's art was only one of their functions. Then, as now, naval officers were military leaders in command of men. One of their most important functions was to fight an enemy, to lead their crew into battle and, if necessary, to board a hostile ship in a hand-to-hand fight until it struck [its colours].[6] Moreover, in times of peace as in times of war, naval officers came frequently into contact with representatives of other countries. They were expected to know one or two foreign languages, to act as the representatives of their own country with firmness, dignity and a certain amount of diplomatic tact, and to behave according to the rules of what were then regarded as good breeding and civility.

In short, an officer of the old navy had to unite in his person some of the qualities of an experienced craftsman with those of a military gentleman.

At first glance, this combination of duties may seem neither surprising nor problematic. In the course of the twentieth century 'gentleman' has become a vague general term referring to conduct rather than social rank. It may be applied to manual workers, to master craftsmen and noblemen alike. During the seventeenth and eighteenth centuries, however, it had a very much stricter social meaning. It was, during the formative period of the naval profession, the distinguishing mark of men from the upper and some portions of the middle classes, setting them off against the rest of the people. Its meaning changed from time to time, usually, with a certain time-lag, in accordance with the changing composition of the House of Commons. But whatever else it meant at a given time, those who worked with their hands, whether master craftsmen or labourers, were always excluded from the ranks of gentlemen. For a gentleman, even the mere suspicion that he had done manual work at any time during his life was degrading.

Pepys's often quoted remark to the effect that among naval officers the seamen were not gentlemen and the gentlemen not sea-men, therefore, was more than the elegant *bon mot* of a Stuart wit.[7] It was the pointed expression of one of the gravest practical problems confronting naval administrators and naval officers throughout the early history of the naval profession. Gentlemen could not learn the art and craft of a seaman without feeling that they had lowered themselves in the eyes of the world. Experienced seamen, on the other hand, who had learned their trade in the only way in which it could be learned, starting early in life as seamen's apprentices, were not regarded as gentlemen; they lacked, or were thought to lack, some of the qualities of prowess, good breeding, military leadership and diplomatic tact, considered indispensable attributes of people who were in command of military operations and who came frequently into contact with foreign officers mostly of noble birth. For the proper functioning of a military fleet of sail it was necessary that its officers should possess some of the qualities of both military gentlemen and seamen. Yet how could one expect to reconcile on board ship social and professional functions which on land appeared wholly incompatible?

The fusion of the duties of seamen and gentlemen as we find it later in the history of the naval profession was, therefore, not the simple and obvious arrangement which it appears to be if one applies to it the social concepts of our time. It was the outcome of a long drawn out struggle and a process of trial and error lasting for more than a century. From the time of Elizabeth to that of Queen Anne and even longer those responsible for the navy wrestled with this problem without much immediate success. Very special conditions, and conditions prevailing in England, and partly in Holland, alone of all the Western European countries, made it possible gradually to overcome these difficulties to some extent. And both the difficulties and the resulting conflicts themselves, as well as the manner in which they were slowly solved, were responsible for some of the most outstanding characteristics of the English naval profession. But in order to understand these developments, it is necessary to cast one's mind back to the social attitudes and standards of that period and to visualise the problems inherent in the growth of the naval profession as they presented themselves to people of that age, not as they appear to us according to the social distinctions and ideals of our own.

THE GROWING INTERDEPENDENCE OF
MARINERS AND MILITARY

In the Middle Ages England did not have a navy in the proper sense of the word. The same military personnel were used for warfare on land and at sea, the same ships for fighting and for trading or fishing. Sea-battles, even in the [English] Channel, were comparatively rare. If they occurred they were fought by land armies assembled on ships in almost the same manner as battles on land. The seamen provided transport; the knights and their followers did the fighting. The association between the two groups was purely temporary. It would have hardly occurred to a noble knight to take over professionally some of the duties and responsibilities of a master mariner.

The situation changed gradually at the time of the great discoveries. During that period, all European countries bordering on the Channel and the Atlantic – with the exception of Germany, weakened by inner dissensions – were drawn, one after the other, into the struggle for domination of the newly discovered sea routes and for possessions overseas. To hold her own England, like her rivals, had to develop her maritime resources. The growing strength of some of her neighbours along the coastline opposite to hers threatened not only her sea communications, but also her security at home. England, for her part, with her growing strength threatened her neighbours on the other side of the Channel and the Spanish seas. The emergence of a new power system all around the Western European seas and the spiral of power rivalry forced all these countries into a contest: it compelled them to fight, to expand, to become what we call imperialist powers, and to go on fighting till one or the other was defeated and fell back. There was no escape from its impact. Like her rivals and allies, England had only the choice to expand or to become dependent on others.

Under the pressure of this steadily expanding sea rivalry, many requirements of these countries and the corresponding techniques

33

transformed themselves more rapidly than before. It became necessary to reorganise fleet and military forces; accordingly, similar
problems of adjustment arose in all these countries. But as their
strategic position and their political and social constitution were
different, the degree, the speed and the method of adjustment varied
a good deal.

In England, the military forces, formerly used indiscriminately for
fighting on land and at sea, divided into land forces and sea forces. The
old sailing fleet, used as the occasion demanded for trading or for
fighting, developed gradually into two more specialised branches,
one mainly commercial, the other mainly military in character.
Specialised branches of fleet and army, drawn together and finally
merged into one, formed in course of time a new specialised
establishment, a military fleet which became known as the navy.

At the same time, these two moves gradually gave rise to a new
profession, that of naval officers. The growing power rivalry brought
about what one might traditionally call a 'division of labour'. In actual
fact, differentiation went hand in hand with integration, specialisation with fusion, transforming not only the labour, but the whole
social functions of people. It was not simply that mariners specialised
for service in a military establishment, and that military gentlemen
attached themselves more permanently to the fleet. The new depar-
ture in maritime warfare created the need for people who in a new
specialised form were seamen and military men at the same time.

However, while it was difficult enough to master the technical
problems raised by the drive for larger and larger ships for specialised [use in] warfare,[b] while people learned slowly and painfully to
build two-deckers and three-deckers with more and more guns, the
solution of the human problems brought about by these changes
proved if anything even more difficult. Two sets of people, mariners
and military gentlemen, who belonged to very different spheres of
life and who in the past had had few professional contacts with each
other, were as a result of these developments forced to collaborate

34

more closely and for longer periods than they had done before. A definite pattern of teamwork embracing both sets did not exist and could not exist at this stage unless an outside authority were strong enough to impose it, as in France and Spain. In England, in that situation, status-battles and a struggle for position were unavoidable. Thrown together by circumstances beyond their power, both groups tried to preserve in their new relationship their traditional mode of life and the professional standards to which they were accustomed. Both failed, and resented it.

In France and Spain, the growing interdependence of these two groups produced very similar problems. But the solution was, at one time or another, imposed from above. Open conflicts between seamen and gentlemen were hardly ever allowed to develop. They were suppressed by strict and immovable regulations. The two groups never, therefore, became fully integrated. Nor did military and nautical functions amalgamate. Noblemen and gentlemen remained in essence military gentlemen and nothing else. It was quite unthinkable that they should pass for a time through a training akin to that of a craftsman; or that craftsmen should become in any respect their equals. They continued, in fact, up to the French Revolution and even longer, to regard and to conduct themselves more or less as specialised detachments of the land army. Professional seamen continued to provide transport for soldiers. The social distance between the two groups was so great that neither feud nor fusion could ensue.

In England, on the other hand, with its different social and political organisation, men from both groups became for a time naval officers. Collaboration between the two groups was closer than in France and Spain; undisguised tensions and open feuds were more frequent; they persisted from Elizabeth's time to that of William of Orange. As a result, there gradually emerged a new division and hierarchy of duties comprising both groups, and these duties were both military and nautical in character.

35

AXIS OF TENSIONS

The initial relation between the two groups was unequivocal: both knew their place. During part of the sixteenth century, the professional seamen were still undisputed masters in their own field. The King, like other shipowners, usually left each of his ships in the care of a master mariner and his associates. The leading corporation of ship's masters, the 'Brotherhood of the most glorious and undivided Trinity' at Deptford-sur-Strand, was, during part of this century, in charge of the Crown Depots at Deptford and of the 'Navy Royall' generally. It was this Corporation, the Trinity House, which selected the master for each of the King's ships. The master, on his part, brought his own 'gang' together, including other craftsmen officers like boatswain, master carpenter, master gunner and cook. They formed the permanent staff of the ship.

The captain, on the other hand, was 'lawfully chosen by a General'.[8] He in turn was 'to make choice of his lieutenant'.[9] And at the end of the journey both left the ship. They, the military officers, were appointed temporarily as the occasion arose.

However, when in the course of the sixteenth century military operations at sea became more frequent, and particularly after the exploits of privateers like Hawkins and Drake had opened before the youth of England new prospects of fame and wealth, young gentlemen were attracted in greater numbers to the sea.[10] From that time on, for more than a century, two groups of officers existed in the navy, with few interruptions, side by side. They were known by such names as 'land captains' and 'sea captains', or 'gentlemen commanders' and 'seamen commanders';[11] the latter, after the Restoration, became also known as tarpaulin commanders or tarpaulins.[12] But whatever their names, in their own time the differences between the two groups were obvious. Later generations often forgot or misunderstood what may have appeared to them as a strange and incomprehensible state of affairs. Their contemporaries took it for granted; they could

36

always tell to which of these two groups a particular naval officer belonged. For although men from both groups, at least nominally, performed the same functions in the navy, often had the same rank, and competed to some extent for the same positions, they differed with regard not only to their professional training but also to their social descent.

The seamen commanders, although in details their careers varied a good deal, had this in common, that they were craftsmen or 'artists'. They had all started as ship's boys early in life; they had served their apprenticeship on board ship, usually for seven years. Whether they had done so in a merchantman or in a man-of-war made little difference; nor did it very much matter whether later in life they had changed from one to the other. In course of time, with the due consent of the shipmasters' corporation, they had become masters – slowly and by degrees if they had nothing but their merits to speak for them, more easily and quickly if they had money or friends to help them. Then they had procured, by chance or by choice, appointment as commander of one of the King's ships, usually, at the beginning, one of the smaller vessels such as a frigate or a fifth rate, or perhaps of a merchant ship enlisted in the King's service during a war. And if they were exceptionally brave or lucky, there was, in principle, nothing to prevent them from rising to the position of an admiral.

The 'gentlemen commanders', on the other hand, came to their command much in the same way as other military officers. There was no question for them of going through an apprenticeship or of learning the trade of an ordinary seaman. While a tarpaulin commander might have passed 'through all the offices and degrees in a ship',[13] before he had become a commander in the King's service, for gentlemen, newcomers as they were to the sea, no comparable series of steps, no regular method of training for the sea existed in Elizabeth's time; and all attempts made during the seventeenth century to establish a similar training and a corresponding series of steps for them

37

more or less failed, mainly because one could hardly hope to attract young gentlemen to the navy by forcing upon them a training incompatible with their status and honour – a training, that is, together with young craftsmen apprentices or at least similar to theirs.

In a small number of cases, gentlemen learned the seamen's art by sharing for a time the hard and rough life of professional seamen. Like [Sir William] Monson or [Sir Henry] Mainwaring, they became privateers or pirates.[14] As a rule, all that was required of a gentleman in order to qualify for a commission in the navy was a few sea voyages as volunteer or in a similar capacity which involved no regular training. It was only in the early eighteenth century that a post and station in the career of young mariners, the post of a midshipman, finally developed into a regular training station reserved for young gentlemen. By then, however, the dividing line between those who were, and those who were not, regarded as gentlemen had slightly shifted its place in the social spectrum.

During the seventeenth century, therefore, many gentlemen went to the sea with little sea experience, procuring appointments by favour or purchase. They were, as Monson wrote, 'Captains who only take upon them that name holding it a maxime that they need not experience'.[15] In the same vein, Pepys half a century later, still struggling not too successfully with the same problem, remarked upon the Elizabethan navy rather wistfully:

> Observe . . . that in '88, though there was a nobleman Admiral, they were fain to make two plain tarpaulins, Drake and Hawkyns, their Vice- and Rear-Admirals notwithstanding there were a great many men of quality in the fleet. . . . But of what service their inexperience could be (more than to shew their prowess) is easy to be judged.[16]

The marked difference between the professional training and career of these two groups of officers was, in other words, closely connected with an equally marked difference in their social antecedents.

38

The seamen captains came as a rule from what one might call the urban middle and lower classes. They belonged to the mass of the common people comprising, at that time, wealthy merchants as well as poor craftsmen and artisans. The gentlemen captains on the other hand were courtiers, or at least men with court connections. Like other people moving in court society they came for the greater part from nobility and gentry. Even if they were of middle-class descent, as sometimes happened, life at court conferred on them a special social status. For members of court society formed a group apart. They distinguished themselves from members of other social groups not only by their real or pretended influence and power derived from close contacts with those who ruled the land, but also by their manners and ambitions, their virtues and vices and their whole mode of life.

Thus the distinction made in the seventeenth century between gentlemen captains and seamen captains in the navy was the equivalent of that made in society at large between men of quality and men of mean birth. It was closely connected with that made, particularly in London, between courtiers and citizens. On land, these classes of people were separated by a wide social gulf. At the outbreak of the civil war, most courtiers and citizens belonged to opposite camps; and the seamen of the navy joined hands with the citizens in protecting parliament.[17] Ashore, they lived in different worlds. Courtiers could hardly admit common people to their acquaintance on terms of equality, let alone of intimacy, without lowering themselves. Yet in the navy men from both groups, gentlemen and seamen, were forced into closer contacts. There, different in social rank as they were, they often held positions of equal professional rank; it could even happen that the roles were reversed and that gentlemen became the subordinates of their social inferiors.

Obviously, this situation was liable to give rise to tensions and conflicts. In order to see it in perspective, one has to remember how different were the social divisions of that period from those of the

39

nineteenth and twentieth centuries. Wealth, in the seventeenth century, certainly counted for much; but birth and upbringing still took precedence over wealth as factors of social rank, and caste over class. In the course of the nineteenth and twentieth centuries social life revolved more and more around tensions and conflicts between middle and lower classes. Corresponding social tensions were certainly not absent during the seventeenth century, but they were still overshadowed by those between the middle and lower classes on the one hand and the upper classes on the other.

From the seventeenth century on, the upper layers of the commercial classes drew nearer to the upper classes; craftsmen and artisans, on the other hand, people engaged in manual work, sank lower in the social scale; and from the latter part of the eighteenth century onwards the chief dividing line of society, the main axis of tensions, shifted more definitely to the commercial and industrial section of the population, dividing it into two camps, the working classes and the middle classes. In the seventeenth century, the line of demarcation between the richer and the poorer sections of the commercial classes was still less sharply drawn. The differences within these classes, great enough in themselves, were small compared to those separating all these groups together from the upper classes and particularly from court society.

SOCIAL ORIGINS OF TARPAULIN COMMANDERS

The relationship between gentlemen and seamen in the navy was greatly influenced by that between the broader strata of English society to which they belonged. Gentlemen who came as officers on board ship naturally continued as best they could to live in the style to which they were accustomed. Towards seamen, they assumed as a matter of course those attitudes of superiority which had become second nature with them in their relation with people of inferior social rank.[18] They were, in short, separated by a wide gap from the rest of the ship's company.

The social distance between seamen captains and their subordinates was, by comparison, small. A seaman captain was not above dining with his subaltern officers. He might, as Sir William Booth did, sleep for years on deck, 'with nothing over him but a tarpaulin, that his seamen be the better contented'.[19] If he took his young son on a journey, we might find the captain's son learning, playing and being whipped together with the children of boatswain and carpenter.[20] And unless the captain had more money, his son's chances in life were probably not very different from those of his playmates.

Nor was there any great difference between the social status of a seaman commander in the navy and the commander of a merchantman. When the middle and lower classes became more differentiated and the gap between the naval and the merchant service widened, the officers of the former came as a rule from a higher social stratum than those of the latter. At the end of the seventeenth century, we can still find in the same family one son a captain in the navy, another master of a merchant ship.[21] We can find officers of the navy taking over posts as masters in the merchant service, masters of merchantmen getting commissions in the navy. Even the mate of a merchantman could say that he 'considered himself full equal of any man holding the King's commission'.[22]

The antecedents and family connections of seamen commanders show the same pattern. Some of them were sons or brothers of well-to-do merchants. Captain Thomas Best, for instance, who was 'bred to the sea' in the usual manner, procured the command of a ship with his father's help, fought in 1612 as an East India trader in the once-famous action off Swally (at the mouth of the Surat river) against a superior Portuguese force, and as a fairly wealthy man left the East India trade for the King's service. Wars, or the threat of wars, always induced the government to employ a considerable number of merchant ships. 'The owners and commanders of ships so taken up by

41

the government were often employed to command them for the Crown.'[23] This was one of the many ways in which merchants, shipowners or ship's masters might become naval captains. Sir Thomas Allin,[24] a native of Lowestoft, appears to have been originally a merchant and shipowner. At the outbreak of the civil war he adhered like his native town to the King. In 1665, he was knighted and appointed Admiral of the Blue[25] under Lord Sandwich. In the navy of the Commonwealth, former merchants, shipowners and ships' masters played an even more prominent part. Richard Deane, James Peacock, Nehemiah Bourne, Richard Badiley – they all, apparently, had gained some sea experience as merchants or shipowners before they became captains, vice-admirals or admirals in the Commonwealth navy. Giles Penn, a captain in the navy, was at another time of his life consul for the English trade in the Mediterranean. His eldest son became an opulent merchant in Spain; his youngest son William, born at Bristol in 1621, served 'with his father from a boy, in various mercantile voyages',[26] became an admiral in the time of the Commonwealth, served in the same capacity under Charles II and was knighted for his services.

Many other tarpaulin commanders came from a stock of craftsmen. There were sons of master mariners or master gunners who in course of time had followed in their fathers' footsteps. Penn, for instance, while still a master, had trained, and taught to write, one George Leake, who himself had been 'taken to sea by his own father while a very little boy and bred by times to do anything of a boy's work as Penn was too'.[27] George Leake later became well known as a master gunner. He was the father of Admiral Sir John Leake.

The texture of that large social group from which the seamen commanders came was in many ways different from that of any comparable group of a fully developed industrial society. If one applies to it present-day labels, for instance [the label] 'middle classes', one must not lose sight of the fact that craftsmen and artisans, people who worked, or who had worked, with their own hands, could be found not only in its lower, but also in its higher layers, that its ranks shaded over imperceptibly into what we might call the 'lower classes', and that by far the greater part of the members of this group were not regarded and did not regard themselves as gentlemen.[28]

In the majority of cases the seamen commanders probably came neither from the richest nor from the poorest section of the common people. The small group of merchant princes, people like Sir Thomas Smythe or William Cockayne of the East India Company, certainly knew more profitable ways of employing their time than commanding a man-of-war. For a poor lad without friends or family influence, on the other hand, it was not very easy to rise above the subordinate positions on board ship. In order to obtain the more profitable place of a master, it was usually necessary to have either a benevolent patron or some money of one's own to pay for the appointment. The detailed description by Edward Barlow[29] of his struggle for advancement from the station of mate to that of master during the later half of the seventeenth century, shows how difficult it was for a man starting without patron or money to obtain the command of a merchant ship or to rise in the King's service.

However, this money barrier was certainly not insuperable. In fact, quite a number of people who came from the poorer sections of the commercial classes, from the 'lower classes' as we might call them, rose to the command of a man-of-war.

Among them the best known is probably Sir Cloudesley Shovel (c.1650–1707)[30] who was apparently a shoemaker's apprentice before he went to the sea as a cabin boy under Sir Christopher Myngs (1625–66)[31] and later under Sir John Narborough (1640–88), two other tarpaulin commanders who in course of time became admirals. He is sometimes remembered as the exceptional case of a man becoming admiral who had 'crept in at the hawse-hole', who in other words had started as a simple seaman before the mast. However, although exceptional qualities enabled him to become an admiral, up to his appointment as captain his career was the normal career of

43

a tarpaulin commander. Among his colleagues, Sir David Mitchell (1650(?)–1710) made his start as apprentice on a Leith trading smack, and was later a mate in the Baltic trade; during the second Dutch war,[32] he was pressed into the navy, distinguished himself, was made second lieutenant in 1677, lieutenant in 1680, and captain in 1684. According to the *Biographia Navalis*[33] he was 'probably not employed during King James, as well from his known aversion to the Catholic faith as from having been one of those who first repaired to the Prince of Orange'. High in William's favour, he became in 1693 Rear Admiral of the Blue and Groom of the Bedchamber. Vice-Admiral John Benbow started according to some writers as a waterman's boy,[34] according to others as a butcher's apprentice.[35] He ran away to the sea and went through the usual training of the professional seaman. In 1678, we find him as master's mate, in 1679 as master in the King's service; then for many years as master, and perhaps as owner, in command of a merchant ship; then again in the navy as third lieutenant under Captain David Mitchell at the Battle of Beachy Head (1689) and again in 1692 at the Battle of La Hogue. In 1693 he was in command of a flotilla of bomb vessels and fire ships, served as Rear Admiral in 1695 and, in 1701, as Commander-in-Chief in the West Indies. He successfully fought the French under Du Casse off Cartagena in 1702 although deserted by the other ships of his squadron and died shortly after of his wounds. He has been described as 'a plain downright seaman', who 'spoke and acted upon all occasions without any respect of persons and with the outmost freedom'.[36] His son was like himself 'bred to the sea'. He went to the East Indies in 1701 as a fourth mate.[37]

SOCIAL ORIGINS OF GENTLEMAN COMMANDERS

Both the family background and the career of a gentleman commander were quite different. Some of them, like Lord Howard of
Effingham and the other Howards, were noblemen, courtiers and
military officers of the highest rank. They took over the command of
a naval army in the same way as any other military command relying
for all marine problems entirely on professional mariners.

Others were noblemen and gentlemen, impoverished or poor
according to their standards, who were first attracted to the sea by
the hope of restoring their fortune – people like Thomas Cavendish
(1560–92) who was in the words of Campbell

> a gentleman descended from a noble family of Devonshire and
> possessed of a very plentiful estate which he being a man of wit and great
> good humour hurt pretty deeply by his expences at court. Upon this he
> took it into his head to repair his shattered fortunes at the expence of the
> Spaniards with which view he built two ships from the stocks . . . and
> sailed from Plymouth on the twenty first of July 1586.[38]

Others came from the landed gentry, younger sons usually, or
sons of younger sons, with a courtier as patron, people like Vice-
Admiral Aylmer (1653–1727), second son of Sir Christopher Aylmer
of Balrath in the county of Meath, who was page to the Duke of
Buckingham when a boy, on the Duke's recommendation got a place
as volunteer on one of the King's ships, became lieutenant in 1678,
commander of a sloop in 1679, captain of a second rate in 1690, and
vice-admiral and Commissioner of the Navy in 1694.[39] Admiral
Edward Russell (1653–1727), later Earl of Orford, was the son of a
younger brother of the first Duke of Bedford.[c] Admiral George
Churchill (1654–1710), son of Sir Winston Churchill (1620–88),[40]
was a younger brother to John, first Duke of Marlborough. Sir Ralph
Delaval, Sir George Rooke and many other gentlemen commanders
belonged to the same category.

45

Others again were the sons and relatives of people who held court offices. The father of Sir George Ayscue was Gentleman of the Privy Chamber to Charles I. Edward Legge, father of George Legge, later Lord Dartmouth, was Groom of the Bedchamber to Charles I; his grandmother was a sister of the first Lord Buckingham.

A small number of the gentlemen commanders were sons of what we would now call 'professional men'. But in most cases their fathers were professional men in the King's service or at any rate in close contact with the court. Edward Herbert, the father of Admiral Herbert, was a gentleman of the long robe.[41] He acted as Attorney General to Charles I, attached himself in exile to the Duke of York and was later appointed Lord Keeper of the Great Seal. Admiral Killigrew was the son of a clergyman. But his family had court connections for more than two generations. His great-grandfather was a Groom of the Privy Chamber of Queen Elizabeth, his grandfather a courtier and MP. His father's sister, Lady Shannon, was one of the mistresses of Charles II. His father, Dr Henry Killigrew, was at the outbreak of the civil war chaplain to the King's army, later chaplain to the Duke of York. Killigrew himself was by upbringing a courtier and a gentleman. He received his first commission after a short service as volunteer.

In order to see the difference more clearly one need only compare Admiral Killigrew's family background with that of a tarpaulin commander, Sir John Berry, vice-admiral under Lord Dartmouth in 1683, whose father was also a clergyman. However, Berry's father was a country vicar, apparently turned out of his living, plundered, and impoverished during the civil war, who died leaving a widow with nine children and little to live on. John Berry, his second son,[42] 17 years old when his father died, went to Plymouth, bound himself apprentice to a merchant, part-owner of several ships, went to sea and learned the trade of a professional seaman in the ordinary way. With the help of some friends, he obtained the place of a boatswain on a ketch of the Royal Navy, and worked his way up from this place, step by step, to that of lieutenant, captain, vice-admiral and Commissioner of the Navy. Pepys knew him well; in his notes from the Tangier expedition in 1683 he left us records of the conversations he had during that journey with Sir John Berry and another distinguished tarpaulin commander, Sir William Booth, who was captain of the expedition's flagship. Like everybody else, Pepys regarded Berry not as a gentleman, but as a professional seaman. Thus, Admiral Killigrew and Sir John Berry, although they were sons of clergymen, came in fact from very different social classes,[43] and belonged to different groups of officers in the navy.

Very occasionally, it happened that men of common birth pretended to the role and status of gentlemen commanders; but, in these cases too, court patronage and familiarity with the outlook and manners of courtiers seems to have been an essential condition. Pepys made a note that according to Sir William Booth 'there are four or five captains which he knows to have been footmen, companions of his own footman, who now reckon themselves among the fine fellows and gentlemen captains of the fleet'. And Pepys added as an afterthought: 'it makes me reflect upon it that by the meaning of gentlemen captains is understood everybody that is not a bred and understanding seaman.'[44]

We know of a few gentlemen who learned the trade of a seaman more or less in the manner of their social inferiors. Sir William Monson,[45] for instance, well known as one of the Elizabethan privateer commanders and as author of the *Naval Tracts*, ran away to sea, probably in 1585, after some years at Balliol College, Oxford, and learned the trade of a seaman for a time in the same hard and rough manner as an ordinary sailor. In 1587, he took the command of a privateer ship, entered the naval service and served first as volunteer and, shortly after, under the patronage of the Earl of Cumberland, apparently as vice-admiral. He took his MA at Oxford in 1594, served in 1596 as captain, and later as Essex's flag captain, in the navy, was knighted after his expedition to Cadiz and acquired fame and wealth

47

when he captured a rich prize in Cezimbra Bay. He had family connections with the court of both Elizabeth and James I. His elder brother was one of the Queen's Chancellors and one of the King's Master Falconers. Monson combined in fact the training and experience of a professional seaman with those of a gentleman and courtier.

But hybrids of this type were not very numerous even in Elizabeth's time when social mobility was comparatively great. They became rarer still under the Stuarts. People spoke more and more openly of seamen and gentlemen as of two different classes of naval officers. And after the civil war class-consciousness was so acute that, in naval circles, and to some extent in the country at large, everybody took the distinction between gentlemen commanders and seamen commanders for granted.

One cannot say with any degree of precision how many naval officers belonged at a given time to each of these two categories.[46] The proportion changed with the changing requirements of the navy and the general policy of the government. But one can say that from the end of the sixteenth to the beginning of the eighteenth century both groups were represented in the navy in numbers sufficient to prevent one of them from dominating the development of the naval profession and from fashioning it alone in accordance with its own standards, traditions and interests. It was in fact the precarious equilibrium and the recurrent tug-of-war between these two groups, reflecting as it did the balance of forces in the country at large, which dominated the history of the naval profession during these early stages of its development.

THE INITIAL CONFLICT AS A BASIC FEATURE
OF A NASCENT INSTITUTION

In retrospect, one may find it difficult, at first, to visualise a profession in which people of different social rank and different professional training worked together as colleagues and, at the same time, struggled with each other as rivals.

However, the naval profession of the sixteenth and seventeenth centuries was certainly not the only profession in which two different social and professional groups, for a time, worked and struggled with each other. Early in the twentieth century the personnel of the rudimentary air force, for instance, was recruited partly from men with the outlook of aviators and partly from military officers. In that case too it was necessary to co-ordinate the work of two sets of people of different mentality and, to some extent, of different social antecedents. But the dispute between them was short, and the rivalry restrained.

Nor are situations of this type confined to the history of military professions. Today, for instance, two groups with different social antecedents and different professional qualifications are sharing with each other the management of state industries. People in charge of these industries are recruited partly from the middle classes and partly from men of working-class descent.[47]

It would not be difficult to find other examples of this kind in past and present. In fact, a similar phase, an initial antagonism and struggle for position between rival groups, may be found in the early history not only of professions, but of almost every institution. If one attempted to work out a general theory of the genesis of institutions one would probably have to say that the initial conflict is one of the basic features of a nascent institution.

One can go still further: one can say that similar status-battles and struggles for position, longer or shorter as the case may be, can be found whenever individuals, initially independent, are about to

49

merge into a group, or smaller groups into a larger.[48] In that sense, the tensions and conflicts between soldiers and mariners, between gentlemen and seamen in the history of the naval profession, may serve as a simple model for other more complex conflicts and struggles in the history of mankind. They were group-tensions and institutional conflicts – that is, inherent in the group-situation of these men and caused by the institutional pattern of their relationships and functions – as distinct from primarily personal tensions and conflicts between people caused for instance by paranoiac or sadistic tendencies or, more generally, by inner conflicts of individuals. For that reason, they reproduced themselves over many generations although the individuals changed.

The detailed account of this struggle and of the gradual emergence of a more unified profession must be left to separate studies. However, the study of the social characteristics of these two groups already gives some clues to the problems which had to be solved before this struggle could come to an end, and to the difficulties which stood in the way of a solution.

The problem first made itself felt, as far as we know, in the time of Elizabeth. As early as 1578, during his voyage of circumnavigation, Drake spoke of the quarrels between gentlemen and mariners and stressed how necessary it was for both groups to work together. More than a century later, in 1683, Pepys made a note on a discussion he had had with Sir William Booth and others on the same subject and wrote that they

> do agree with me that gentlemen ought to be brought into the Navy, as being men that are more sensible of honour than a man of meaner birth (though here may be room to examine whether as great actions in honour have not been done by plain seamen, and as mean by gentlemen, as any others and this is worth enquiring) but then they ought to be brought up by time at sea. . . . And then besides the good they would do for the King and Navy, by their friends at Court they would themselves

espouse the cause of the seamen and know what they deserve, and love them as part of himself; and the seamen would be brought to love them rather more than one of themselves because of his quality, he being otherwise their fellow seaman and labourer.[49]

And in 1694 the Marquis of Halifax again referred, in his *Rough Draught of a New Model at Sea*, to 'the present Controversie between the Gentlemen and the Tarpaulins'; he still discussed the question 'Out of what sort of Men the Officers of the Fleet are to be chosen . . .',[50] and gave it as his opinion that 'there must be a mixture in the Navy of Gentlemen and Tarpaulins'.[51]

From the time of Drake to that of Halifax, a compromise between the two groups and an integration of the two appeared to many people as the ideal solution. However, as in many other cases, no one quite knew how this ideal was to be attained. Neither Drake, nor Pepys, nor Halifax produced a durable scheme by means of which it could be put into practice. For as the seamen were not gentlemen and the gentlemen not seamen, how was it possible to devise a unified scheme for the training and promotion of naval officers satisfactory to both groups?

2

Tensions and Conflicts

INTRODUCTION

Tensions and conflicts owing to the presence of two different groups in the navy, of military gentlemen and professional seamen, made themselves felt, so far as one can see, under Elizabeth and the early Stuarts. The struggle ceased under the Commonwealth, when gentlemen officers more or less disappeared from the navy, flared up again with increased intensity after the Restoration, continued under William III and came to an end, at least as an open feud, in the early part of the eighteenth century. From it emerged the general framework of the naval profession as we know it, namely a firm hierarchy of naval offices, embodying to some extent the functions and characteristics of both groups, with a unified mode of training and specific line of promotion for different classes of officers.

On the whole, it was not a very spectacular struggle. Unlike wars, or even civil wars, it did not culminate in any great and decisive action which one can name. Its manifestations were often nothing more than rows and quarrels of a very ordinary kind such as almost everybody occasionally encounters in their everyday life. Perhaps for that reason, it has attracted comparatively little attention among historians.

Nor can one assume that those involved in quarrels of this kind were themselves always aware of the wider implications of this struggle. Most of them felt antagonistic to people from the other group probably without realising that their antagonism had been brought about, in the last resort, by a wide nexus of political, social and technical changes in England as well as the Atlantic group of countries as a whole, and more specifically by the changing conditions of sea warfare. They were at best only dimly aware that their hostile feelings for each other were due to the peculiar nature of their relationship rather than to inherently opposed qualities of the other group. Nor was it easy for them to see that these conflicts were part of the genesis of a growing profession. In most cases they simply experienced individual representatives of the other group as irritants, arousing, according to circumstances and temperament, annoyance, anger, contempt, hatred or fury. At the same time, practical considerations compelled people from both groups quite often to collaborate. While quarrelling they became in fact more and more dependent on each other; and their growing interdependence caused them to quarrel. It was this simultaneity of antagonism and co-operation which gave to this struggle, as to others of its kind, its peculiar character.

Contemporary records of these feuds are scanty.[1] New material may come to light once the general pattern of the struggle as such stands out more clearly. But in all probability most of the incidents, great and small, born from this antagonism between gentlemen and seamen have never been recorded; or, if recorded, can no longer be recognised as such.

Still, the gist of the arguments used by both sides has been handed on to us. Together with scattered reports from a small number of incidents and from other factual evidence, they enable us to gain a fairly clear picture of the conditions which gave rise to these dissensions and of the course and pattern of the struggle itself.

THE FORMATIVE CONFLICT: DRAKE AND DOUGHTY

The first major incident of which we know in this long drawn out
tug-of-war between seamen and gentlemen occurred in 1577–8,
during Drake's journey round the world. It is perhaps the best docu-
mented episode of its kind. In many ways, it is representative of the
initial stage in the development of the naval profession in which
members of two different classes came first into closer contact on
board ship. It affords us a glimpse, as do few others, of their feelings
and attitudes towards each other. For that reason alone it is worth
considering its course and climax in some detail.[2]

In November 1577[3] a small fleet sailed from Plymouth under
the leadership of Francis Drake, ostensibly for Alexandria. Only
Drake himself and some of the other leading men knew that their
real goal was the discovery of unknown lands in the South Pacific not
belonging to the King of Spain, but, so one hoped, as rich in silver
and gold as the Spanish dominions. Drake's idea was apparently to
reach the South Pacific via the Straits of Magellan and if possible to
explore the coast of the unknown Terra Australis of which much had
been heard, but of which nothing certain was known.[4] At the same
time, the expedition had another more immediate aim. Its leading
men hoped to take rich booty from the Spaniards and the Portuguese,
mainly by capturing prizes. Drake had done so before; he had, at that
time, already gained a reputation as privateer; and he and his companions hoped to repeat these exploits. Without this second more
tangible prospect of profit it might have been much harder to find
influential people willing to invest money in such a hazardous
enterprise; and without sufficient capital the whole plan would have
come to nought.

Moreover, an expedition of this kind required the consent of the
court. The attitude of the Queen [Elizabeth] and her councillors
towards this irregular form of warfare depended a good deal on the
political situation. There had been times when they thought it

necessary that the Queen's subjects should keep the peace with Spain and should not irritate the Spanish King by piracy and privateering. Drake had some experience in this matter. Earlier in his life, in 1573, when he returned with his spoils from one of his private expeditions against the Spanish dominions in America, he had been ill received at home. The Queen apparently had disapproved of his exploits. Drake seems to have felt that it might be wiser for him to disappear for a while. And so, after two years of which we have no account, he had taken service with the Earl of Essex who was then trying to suppress an Irish rebellion.

There, in Ireland, Drake had met Thomas Doughty, a gentleman and soldier of some repute who was at that time Essex's secretary. They had become close friends. And together, the two men had planned a new and more ambitious expedition to the southern parts of the American continent and perhaps the Pacific, each contributing something to the execution of the project which the other lacked. Drake, by upbringing a professional seaman,[5] knew all that could be known of sea voyages to America; but he had had few connections with the court; in his dealings with people he had the directness and often the bluntness of the professional seaman and lacked experience of the ways and manners of courtiers. Doughty, on the other hand, by upbringing a gentleman, had, so far as we know, little experience of the sea, but he had court connections and the education necessary for life among courtiers.

When they returned to England, in 1576, the political situation was not unfavourable to their plans. A powerful faction at court pressed for a more aggressive policy towards Spain. One of the Queen's favourite courtiers, Christopher Hatton, who was Captain of the Guards, had taken great interest in their plans. He had made Doughty his secretary. Together with Leicester,[6] Walsingham,[7] the Lord Admiral[8] and others he had formed a syndicate which sponsored and financed the project.[9] Drake had been introduced to the Queen herself;[10] and although she probably did not wish to become publicly associated with a project that would lead to hostile actions against subjects of the King of Spain, she had approved of his plans; in fact, she had become one of the main subscribers of the expedition and had appointed Drake as its head. Thus Drake, who had been left high and dry some years before when the Queen had tried to appease the Spaniards, was now carried to success on a rising wave of more bellicose feelings at court.

Whatever his appointment implied, the scope of his authority – particularly in relation to other leading men – was far from clear. An expedition of this kind was at that time still a comparatively new venture. Not even a uniform name for the office of its leader had established itself by common usage. Sometimes people spoke of Drake, or of his flagship, as 'Admiral', sometimes as 'Captain General' or as 'General', or simply as 'Captain', using now a term specially related to warfare at sea, now others more commonly applied to officers in command of land armies. What is more, among those who followed him on this journey, different sets of people held different opinions in regard to the rights and duties entailed by his assignment.

For on this journey, Drake, as commander-in-chief of a whole fleet sent out by the Queen, was perhaps for the first time in his life at the head of a company which consisted not only of seamen but also of gentlemen and soldiers. He was accompanied by about a dozen gentlemen volunteers who owed their place to one or another member of the sponsoring court syndicate. Many of them, if not all, were 'adventurers', that is, they had been allotted a fixed share in the expected proceeds of the expedition. With one or two exceptions they probably had little sea experience. Most of them had no specific function on board ship apart from fighting. The most prominent among them were John Winter, Drake's second-in-command, who was apparently a relative of Sir William Winter, Surveyor of the Navy and a follower of the Lord Admiral, and Drake's friend, Thomas Doughty, who was the leading soldier of the expedition. Two gentlemen, Thomas and Chester, had been made captains of

56

two of the smaller ships; but the captain's functions, at that stage, were still mainly those of a military officer; he left all matters connected with navigation and with the government of the sailors to the ship's master.

In many respects, the ideas of these gentlemen about the division of authority and the way in which decisions should be taken on this journey differed from those of Drake. Traditions of long standing determined the scope and limits of the authority of the leading seaman in a company of mariners and that of the leading soldier in a company of soldiers. But there were few precedents for the position of a seaman in command of both military and nautical operations, of soldiers *as well as sailors.* The ship's company in fact consisted no longer of one, but of two groups, each with a marked identity and with social standards of its own; it had become a community with strong social divisions. As time went on, these divisions produced tensions; they led to heated arguments and quarrels between seamen and gentlemen generally; and they culminated in a bitter feud between two of the leading men, between Drake himself who was the leading seaman, and Doughty who was the leading soldier. The pull of the situation, as one might call it, was so strong that it transformed friends into enemies.

Drake, when he set out on his expedition to the unknown Terra Australis, seems to have been quite certain that the Queen had entrusted him with the 'absolute command' of the enterprise.[11] He was conscious of being one of the most experienced and successful privateer commanders of his time. He had the self-confidence characteristic of many great leaders of men; he was always quite certain that he could successfully finish whatever he undertook if he were able to lead and the others were willing to follow. Throughout his life, he had never found it easy to bear with rivals; he was always inclined to quarrel, often violently with those who seemed to thwart him.[12] And the seamen's traditions were sufficiently elastic to allow a man of his talents and temperament to assert himself. As long as they were among themselves, the old mariners lived in the form of a rugged democracy characteristic of many small and simple groups, which enabled its leader to act, if necessary, autocratically or even tyrannically as long as he could command the confidence of the majority of his men. In the company of seamen, as far as one can see, Drake never found it difficult to impart to others his self-confidence and to make his own counsel prevail. He had lived among them all his life; he spoke their language; he thoroughly understood their manners and their way of thinking; and so, among mariners, he always could have his own way if he wanted to.

It was less easy for him to gain the ascendancy among gentlemen. In many respects their concept of a leader's personality, and of his rights and duties, differed from that of the seamen. They were used, among themselves, to the observation of certain forms of etiquette and good manners. They were more accustomed to thinking in terms of formal laws and regulations. And although, as a matter of course, they regarded the seamen as their inferiors, they themselves, as gentlemen, expected to be treated more or less as equals by their leader. In that respect, Doughty's attitude was quite clear; and he never changed it. Like the rest of the company, he acknowledged Drake as the official leader of the expedition. But he did not regard himself as Drake's subordinate. He and the other leading gentlemen considered themselves as members of Drake's council. And in relation to his council an admiral was at that time, and for a long time to come, not a ruler free to impose his own decisions on the other members. He did not take any major decision without consulting his council. He was, as a rule, a *primus inter pares*. That, at the best, was Drake's position on this journey as the gentlemen saw it.

The views of the two sides, therefore, with regard to the division of authority and their mutual position in general differed widely. Both were sincerely convinced that their own views agreed with the intentions of the Queen and the authorities at home. But their official assignment, in all likelihood, was less definite than they liked to think.

It left room for contradictory interpretations; it hardly covered the variety of human problems springing up in this novel situation. People could not yet look for guidance and for help against the pressure of their own passions to a well tried code of conduct and to unequivocal rules clearly defining the position of different sets of officers and men in relation to each other. Nor could they rely on a routine method for the handling of quarrels and conflicts. As long as each group had lived by itself, its members were bound by certain traditional ways of dealing with dissension; when they were brought into closer association these methods proved no longer effective. Under these conditions, gentlemen and seamen, isolated on the high seas far from the moderating influence of their homeland, had to work out their own salvation in the primeval way, by means of a struggle.

During the first part of their journey, sailing towards Africa and along the West African coast before turning westwards, Drake and Doughty, whatever they felt, still behaved as friends. There were, as it seems, disagreements. Doughty's implicit assumption that he was his equal probably irritated Drake at least as much as Drake's claim to a superior position irritated Doughty. But both tried to keep their temper. When they captured their first prize, a rich Portuguese ship which they renamed *Mary*, Drake put Doughty in charge as her commander or captain. As Doughty was the leading military officer of the expedition, Drake probably could not do less. But he took the precaution of sending his own brother Thomas together with Doughty to the *Mary*.

It was there that the storm broke. All along, not the least important cause of tensions between seamen and gentlemen was apparently the question of the division of their spoils. On privateer expeditions, the seamen were used to sharing the spoils mainly among themselves. They therefore resented the fact that on this journey they had to share the proceeds of their labour with gentlemen adventurers who, as they saw it, did little work. The capture of their first prize probably gave an edge to these feelings. Soon after they came on board

Doughty and Thomas Drake had a violent quarrel, each accusing the other of having pilfered the cargo. While the battle raged, word was sent to the flagship. Francis Drake hurried on board the *Mary*, and burst out swearing and raging into a torrent of accusations against Doughty. He charged him with trying 'to sap his credit with the fleet', swearing by God's life that he would not suffer it. He knew quite well, he said, that it was not Thomas, but Francis Drake whom he meant covertly to disparage.[13] All the pent up resentment and the suspicions against Doughty which had been mounting in his mind for some time came into the open. He dismissed Doughty from the command of the *Mary* and appointed his brother as captain. It was the first open breach between the two former friends.

Even then, it appears, Drake was neither certain of his power, nor clear about his course of action. Some of the other gentlemen tried to heal the breach; and for a time the two men once more made their peace with each other. Both probably realised that these violent quarrels threatened to disrupt the whole journey. The uncertainty with regard to the right to command and to take decisions made itself felt throughout the company. Nobody quite knew who should give orders and who obey whom. And so, surprisingly enough, while they were sailing across the Atlantic towards South America, the two men changed places. Drake made the journey to Brazil on board the Portuguese prize. Doughty took over the command of Drake's flagship, the *Pelican*. And when he came on board, he assembled the ship's company and tried to restore discipline:

there hath been great travails, fallings out, and quarrels among you and that every one of you have been uncertain whom to obey, because there were many who took upon them to be masters, one commanding to such, another one forbidden, another commanded ... The General by his wisdom and discretion set down order that all things might be better done with peace and quietness. And for that he hath a special care of this place, being his admiral and chief ship and indeed his treasury for the whole fleet. . . . He hath sent me as his friend whom he trusteth to take charge in his place, giving unto me special commandment to signify unto you that all matters by-past are forgiven and forgotten.[14]

But peace did not last long. Suspicions had been blurted out and threats openly vented. When a struggle for leadership has reached that stage, it can rarely be halted by a superficial reconciliation. Whatever the immediate reason, after some time Drake again accused Doughty of trying to blacken his name. While his own feelings against his former friend were growing in intensity, Drake himself, it seems, felt more and more threatened by him. He accused Doughty of 'taking upon himself too great a command'. He charged him with using witchcraft and with planning to murder him. How far all these accusations were true, how far they were figments of Drake's imagination, is hard to say. But they certainly show that rivalry turned, as it often does, friendship into enmity and affection into hatred. From now on Drake fought openly against Doughty.

He had, at that stage, certainly good reasons to feel that the whole expedition might fail unless he could establish unequivocally his own right to command as he understood it. Had he been by upbringing a gentleman, he might have succeeded in winning over the other gentlemen by the strength of his arguments. As it was, being perhaps not articulate enough in manner and speech, he could not play the gentlemen's game in their own way. He lost his temper and became brusque and offensive, and then again conciliatory; and wavering in his attitude he merely increased their resentment; he injured Doughty's pride more and more and strengthened his resolve not to be put out of what he regarded as his rightful place. And the stiffening of Doughty's attitude in turn increased Drake's own fears and suspicions. Constantly thwarted in his designs he felt, rightly or wrongly, that Doughty and his friends were plotting against him and were threatening his life until he could bear it no longer and accused Doughty openly of being a witch and a murderer.

61

It was in that mood that he sent him to a little victualling ship, the *Swan*, virtually as a prisoner.

And there, Doughty, far from holding his tongue spoke out. He had been publicly abused and humiliated by Drake; and so he told everybody who wanted to hear it that Drake owed his present position to him, that it was he who introduced Drake to the members of the Privy Council and who had helped him 'to the Queen's pay', and that then Drake had played him false; for he had allotted him only a small financial share in the expedition which they had planned together thus breaking 'the promise between them'. And he scoffed at Drake's accusations. 'Whosoever did speak against him, he said, he would . . . into their mouths, when he came to England'. And as for being a conjuror and a traitor, he would purge himself of all these accusations in England 'before the better of those who did accuse him . . . to their great shame'. He hinted at secrets of Drake which he knew though he would not divulge them, he said, even if Drake 'should use me very hardly', and yet such a disclosure would 'touch him very much'. Above all he insisted on his rights and on the respect due to him as a gentleman. He knew, he said, with great self-assurance that Drake could not 'cast him off', for he, Thomas Doughty, 'was a gentleman',[15] and Drake was not to do anything without his assent.[16]

That it was not the wisest thing Doughty could do, thus to speak his mind and to attack Drake openly in a company which consisted mainly of seamen, is obvious. But a gentleman of that age was hardly brought up to receive insults with meekness or to act with prudence and self-restraint when challenged to a fight. Like Drake himself, Doughty acted very much in accordance with his role in life; he could hardly help it. Slighted in his honour and humiliated in his self-respect, he spoke out, blind to the feelings of those around him.

They on their part reacted as one might have expected. The seamen were in no mood to listen calmly to these speeches against their leader. The captain of the little flyboat where all this happened was a gentleman named Chester. He and the master, as was usual in the Tudor navy, messed together; and Doughty shared their table as a matter of course. The master, naturally, took Doughty's speeches against Drake in bad part. They quarrelled; one day after dinner Master Sarocold told Doughty to his face that Drake might do well to deal with traitors and enemies to their enterprise as Magellan had done on his journey round the world; he ought to have them hanged. Doughty replied that he knew Drake's authority as well as Drake himself; it was by no means the same as Magellan's. And so, one thing leading to another, they came to blows. The master left the gentleman's table taking his seat among the mariners. And having Doughty in his power he showed his hatred and contempt by keeping him and the other gentlemen on a low diet. He saw to it that the mariners' mess was well provided with food while the gentlemen were given less and less to eat. Doughty tried to reason with Master Sarocold; he reminded him again that he was a gentleman and an adventurer. But the master told him he did not care a fig for him and his adventure: 'when thow comest home to inioye any adventure', he said, 'I will be hanged', and 'Wilt thow have victualles, thow shalt be glade . . . the rather to eate that falls from my tayle on the ankor slooke'.[17] Doughty turned to the Captain, urging him to follow his command, to take the sword and to assert his authority which had been given to him by Drake himself. But his words had little effect. Even had the Captain wished to follow Doughty, confronted as they were by the hostility of all the mariners, they had hardly a chance.

Moreover, while seamen and gentlemen were thus quarrelling on board their little ship, they were caught in a storm and lost sight of the other ships of the expedition. And in their absence Drake was storming and raging against Doughty on board his flagship.

During the whole of their absence [wrote one member of the company], our General never ceased to inveigh against him terming him a conjuror and a witch, and at any time when we had any foul weather he would say that Thomas Doughty had been the occasioner thereof and . . . that it came out of Tom Doughty's capcase . . . and would avouch the same with great oaths which he at no time scanted, they cost him so little.[18]

When after some time the *Swan* succeeded in joining the other ships again, Doughty was brought back to the *Pelican*. Once more he and Drake had a savage row with each other. Doughty could not help dreading the prospect of a long journey in this company; he apparently wished to confine the enterprise to the Atlantic. Drake wanted to sail on to the Pacific in accordance with his original plan. In the end Drake knocked Doughty down and had him tied to the mainmast. Enraged beyond measure, he had evidently decided to make an end of it, and to allow no further opposition to his authority. He led the expedition to the sheltered harbour of Port St Julian in Patagonia. There, 58 years before, Magellan, on the first successful voyage round the globe had executed one of the leading gentlemen of his company. Drake intended, in that respect too, to follow in his footsteps.

The accounts of eyewitnesses about the events in that lonely place near the southern tip of the American continent where, as one of the gentlemen wrote later, 'will was law and reason put into exile'[19] differ again a good deal according to their bias in favour of Drake or of Doughty. What emerges quite clearly is how ineluctably both men had driven each other into a position from which they could neither retreat without fear, nor advance without fighting. Their struggle had followed a pattern which is only too well known. At the outset each man and the group to which he belonged by upbringing and tradition, had probably merely tried to defend what they regarded as their rightful place against the encroachments of the others. But each move of one side, intended as a defence, had been experienced by the other as an attack demanding an even stronger defence. And so, growing on the rebound, the tension had reached a stage where each man and his group felt threatened in their lives by the other, and retaliated as best they could.[20]

64

Once on land, Drake accused Doughty again of having tried to undermine his authority and of having plotted against his life. Doughty asked that he should be sent back to England if such grave accusations were levelled against him, so that he could be tried there in the proper manner 'by Her Majesty's laws'.[21] But Drake would have none of it. He had obviously decided that it was neither safe to send Doughty home, where he had powerful friends, nor possible to continue the journey with a fair prospect of success as long as Doughty was present. He insisted that a jury should be set up and that Doughty should be tried there and then. Doughty again challenged Drake's authority; still undaunted he demanded to see Drake's commission. He had had a lawyer's training; and he was clearly convinced that Drake had no right to try, let alone to execute him. But in Drake's eyes the concern of Doughty and some of the other gentlemen appeared merely as another ruse of these 'crafty lawyers'; he told them 'he did not care for the law'. He was convinced that the Queen had meant to give him all the authority he needed for a successful execution of his journey, whatever she had put in writing. He empanelled a jury; and as the result of their findings was apparently not as conclusive as he wished, he finally assembled the whole company on land. There 'placing himself in a more elevated position than the others, he took out some papers, kissed them, put them on his head, and read them in a loud voice'.[22] He showed them to the others who saw and inspected them. But according to the only detailed report we have of these papers his commission was not among them. When asked he declared he had forgotten it in his cabin.[23] The issue between the two men and their followers had clearly reached a stage where rules laid down by distant authorities were of less importance than their immediate power. It had become a life and death struggle hardly any longer disguised by the trappings of an ordered society. In the end, Drake brushing aside most of the specific charges against Doughty into which the jury inquired, put the broad issue, as he saw it, before his assembled companions:

65

My masters you may see whether this fellow has sought my discredit or not, and what should hereby be meant but the very overthrow of the voyage, at first by taking away my good name . . . and then my life which I being bereaved of what then will you do; you will fain one to drink an other's blood, and so to return again unto your country, you will never be able to find the way thither . . . And if this voyage go not forward, which I cannot see how possible it should if this man live, what a reproach it will be not only unto our country, but especially unto us. Therefore, my masters, they that think this man worthy to die, let them with me hold up their hands and they that think him not worthy to die hold down their hands.[24]

The majority voted in favour of Doughty's death and he was duly executed. The long and bitter struggle for the leadership of the expedition had come to an end. A little later, moreover, the other leading gentleman, John Winter, Drake's vice-admiral, equally dissatisfied with Drake's regime, left the expedition and turned homewards with his own ship, 'full sore against the mariner's mind'. From now on Drake's voice alone counted on this journey. He had established his 'absolute command'.[25]

What the other gentlemen thought and felt when their leaders disappeared from the scene, one can only guess. Drake himself was well aware of the general antagonism between gentlemen and sea-men, and, having won his own struggle with the leading military gentleman of the expedition, he tried to reconcile the two groups. Shortly after Doughty's execution he made his often quoted appeal for collaboration which reads like an epitome of the whole:

Here is such controversy between sailors and gentlemen, and such stomaching between gentlemen and sailors, that it does even make me mad to hear it. But, my masters, I must have it left, for I must have the gentlemen haul and draw with the mariner, and the mariner with the gentlemen. What let us show ourselves all to be of a company, and let us not give occasion to the enemy to rejoice at our decay and overthrow.[26]

66

The solution, at that time already, seemed perfectly clear. Yet the conflict was only at its beginning.

TO HAUL AND DRAW?

Few other episodes show so clearly and vividly as this the initial situation of the two groups whose functions went into the making of the naval profession. It brings to mind the difficulties that had to be overcome before a unified profession could emerge from their encounter.

One can see their predicament.

When the development of sea warfare in the Atlantic, and with it that of fleets specialised for warfare, made it necessary for soldiers and sailors to live together for longer periods and to work together in closer collaboration, each group at first threatened what appeared to the other to be the natural order of things. Each endangered the other's traditional status and self-respect; each curtailed the other's chances of gain and advancement.

At the outset, the mariners, like other craftsmen of that age, still formed a closely-knit group. They were organised in corporations. In that form they governed themselves. As long as the conduct of their own affairs agreed with the general policy of the court, the central authorities rarely interfered with their professional arrangements. In their own sphere of work they thus enjoyed a fairly large measure of independence.

The appearance on board ship of gentlemen connected with the court who aspired to a place of authority ran counter to these traditions. It not only lowered the seamen's prospect of gain, it threatened their independence; they were not used to any supervision by people from a higher social order. And it injured their pride; it was humiliating to see the rule of men of their own kind superseded or curtailed by landsmen. The coming of gentlemen

67

endangered the social standing of the seamen themselves as well as that of their art and craft.

The position of gentlemen in a company of seamen was even less compatible with their traditional standards and status requirements. They claimed for themselves a place of authority in virtue of their fighting experience, their military rank and, generally, their social status. They belonged to, or identified themselves with, the group who governed the country; and so it appeared only natural to them that they should govern the ship. It was the privilege of gentlemen to take the lead in military expeditions on land; they therefore expected as a matter of course to take the lead in military expeditions at sea. Yet, on board ship, they were in many ways dependent on those whom they meant to command. They lacked the seamen's specialised knowledge; most of them were out of their depth at sea; and being less secure in their position than on land they tended all the more to demonstrate their own superiority in language and behaviour. They felt humiliated when the seamen, resentful at the intrusion of landsmen, failed to show the customary marks of respect and submission. Worse still, some of the seamen, former ship's masters like Drake and others, aspired and were in fact appointed to the leading positions in military expeditions. Again and again, in the navy gentlemen found their social inferiors as colleagues and potential rivals. The seamen were needed as captains and even as flag officers because they possessed the specialised knowledge which gentlemen lacked; and as long as the gentlemen officers lacked this knowledge, they could not hope to reserve the commanding positions for men of their own kind.

In fact, gentlemen who went to the sea were caught in a dilemma. In the army, the position of an officer required no specialised training other than that which every gentleman of that age received as a matter of course. In the navy, the corresponding positions required a far more specialised training. But it was a training to which few gentlemen could willingly submit. It involved not only a manner of living unsuitable for noblemen and courtiers,[27] but also manual

68

work; and manual work was taboo.[28] Gentlemen of that age had more or less the same feelings at the prospect of doing the seamen's work as, centuries later, men from the middle classes had at the prospect of doing factory work. In their eyes, the work of a seaman ineradicably bore the stamp and stigma of a lower class; to do it, even for a time, meant losing caste.

In his own circles, it appeared as perfectly natural that society was divided into those who ruled and those who were being ruled, into men of quality who owned the land and were bred to fight and to command, and the masses who were bred to make their living by work. For gentlemen to do the same work as the lower orders, therefore, meant threatening the established order of things. The prohibition against manual work had deep roots in the sentiments of all those brought up as gentlemen. It could not be rescinded merely by rational arguments or practical considerations. It was an essential element of the gentleman's picture of himself; it belonged to the inner code which told gentlemen what to do and what not to do; it formed part and parcel of the 'gentleman ideal'.

Thus, the naval gentlemen of the sixteenth and seventeenth centuries were confronted with two alternatives both equally unsatisfactory according to their standards. They could try to acquire the seamen's specialised skill by doing, at least for a time, the seamen's work. In that case, they infringed the strict code of their own group, and ran the risk of lowering not only their personal status but also that of gentlemen officers in general. Or they could refuse to be trained for the sea more of less in the same manner as professional seamen. In that case they remained utterly dependent on seamen for the navigation and the entire working of the ship. And as it went beyond the power of most gentlemen to violate at sea the social code of their own class as long as it was valid on land, they perpetuated, by their own inability to acquire the seamen's specialised skill, the need for more experienced officers from a lower class – though they resented their presence as a slight to their honour and a limitation of their own chances of employment and promotion; while the seamen officers themselves felt equally resentful, for similar reasons, at the imposition of landsmen.

It was this situation rather than any inherent wickedness of one side or the other which caused, for several generations, tensions, status battles and a general struggle for position between seamen and gentlemen. No group can tolerate without resistance a threat to their status and self-respect; few individuals suffer quietly in the break-up of what they have come to regard as their role in life, for without it in their own mind their life loses its value and its meaning.

Regarded as a step towards greater 'specialisation of labour', the task of merging the functions of sailors and soldiers into one special-ised naval profession might appear simple and straightforward. Seen as a change in group relations affecting not only functions but also human beings, the same process shows a far more complex pattern. Like many other processes of specialisation, it upset the existing status order in one limited field, often at a time when the corresponding division of power in the country at large was still unchanged. Its first impact made the two main groups involved more aware of what they stood to lose by the change than of what they had to gain. Their old role, that of military gentlemen or profes-sional seamen, was meaningful: not only the respect of others, but also their self-respect, were bound up with it. Their new role, that of naval officers, emerged only gradually; at the outset, it was of uncer-tain status, vague in outline and without special emotional signifi-cance. Most officers went into the navy in search of employment or money or adventure. But their standing as gentlemen or professional seamen still meant far more to them than their role as naval officers. Neither group wished to forgo the chances of employment, gain and prestige which the new service offered: but neither was willing to suffer an encroachment upon its traditional functions and privileges.[29] Inevitably frictions became stronger and more frequent, the closer and more permanent their association became.

The struggle during Drake's expedition in 1577 showed for once the seamen in power. It is possible that Drake, having established his own authority, made the gentlemen 'set their hands to a rope' and 'haul and draw with the mariner'. But it certainly was the last thing gentlemen wished to do of their own accord. There are many examples showing the gentlemen's attitude when they had the upper hand. In the time of Charles I, for instance, when gentlemen again went to the sea in greater numbers and gentlemen commanders were often accompanied on their journeys by a considerable number of young gentlemen volunteers who wished to gain sea experience, it could happen that none of them took any part in the seamen's work even during a storm. 'I confess', wrote an anonymous author at that time, referring to these young gentlemen,

> it is most necessary such should go, but not too many in one ship; for if the labour of sixty should lie upon thirty, as many times it does, they are so overcharged with labour, bruises and over-straining themselves; for there is no dallying nor excuses with storms, gust, overgrown seas and ley-shores. They fall sick of one disease or other, and then if the victuals be putrified it endangers all.[30]

Another, referring to the corresponding attitude of the seamen:

> if any will tell me, why the vulgar sort of Seamen hate Landmen so much, either he or I may give the reason, why they are so unwilling to teach them in their Art; whence it is that so many gentlemen go long voyages and return in a manner as ignorant and unable to do their country service as when they went out.[31]

That is not to say that gentlemen and seamen were always at loggerheads. Frequent contacts in the navy left their marks on both. In course of time, each group took over from the other some of its attitudes or some of its skills. Moreover, common sense often

71

induced men from both groups to collaborate as best they could, particularly in a struggle with enemy forces. One should not think that strife was incompatible with amity or rivalry with collaboration. Individually, many gentlemen and seamen were on friendly terms and understood each other well. There were people from both groups who saw that closer collaboration was necessary. But how should one proceed? In what manner should the responsibilities be divided between the leading men from both groups? Who should rule the ship? And who the whole fleet? As long as this relationship remained an association lacking a clear demarcation of functions or a unified order of promotion and ranks, the underlying antagonism was bound to express itself again and again in quarrels and conflicts.

At the same time, it was extremely difficult to remove these causes of strife without deeply offending one or other of the two groups, both at this stage equally indispensable for the proper working of the navy. Under the Commonwealth, naval officers were recruited as far as possible from the ranks of the professional seamen alone. For the rest, the two groups, seamen and gentlemen, now collaborating, now bitterly quarrelling had to work out among themselves a *modus vivendi* however precarious.

It was to this mode of development by trial and error rather than by dictation from above, that the English naval profession owed many of its distinguishing characteristics. For, paradoxically enough, these quarrels and conflicts between seamen and gentlemen were not only the prelude to the gradual amalgamation of some of the functions of both groups, but an essential part of the process of specialisation and integration itself.

CAPTAINS AND MASTERS, LIEUTENANTS AND MASTERS

In one form or the other, the antagonism between gentlemen and seamen affected all members of the two groups. But the struggle itself revolved around two specific issues raised by the unstable relationship between the leading men of both groups.

On board ship it centred on the relationship between the ship's master on the one hand and the captain and his lieutenant on the other. Underlying most of the individual contests between these men was one basic issue: Should gentlemen captains continue as they did initially, to take charge mainly of military operations and the overall direction of the ship, leaving the master virtually in command of the mariners and in charge of navigation? Or should they together with lieutenants become the real rulers of the ship and the masters completely subordinate to their command?

The decision on this issue was ultimately dependent on the outcome of the second very much wider issue which centred on the relative position of seamen officers and gentlemen officers in the navy generally. Leading men from both groups, gentlemen and seamen, were potential competitors for the same naval appointments. The crucial question underlying most of their feuds and dissensions was this: Should both groups have unrestricted access to the commanding positions of the navy, to the posts of captains and flag officers? Or perhaps be admitted to them only in limited numbers?

Both groups had close links with one or other of the social groups who, especially during the seventeenth century, often wrestled and sometimes fought with each other in the country at large. In the last resort, it was the outcome of the wider social and political struggles which finally decided these professional issues, thus determining in a general way the mould in which the naval profession was cast.

The history of the first of these relationships, that between the leading seaman and the leading gentlemen on board ship, throws a good deal of light on the way in which specific naval offices grew into shape. It must be enough here to sketch out briefly its general outline.

In the earlier stages, for example in the Tudor navy, the master in smaller vessels was what he used to be – and in merchantmen of all classes remained – the man in command. In larger ships of the King's or the Queen's fleet, though nominally subordinate to the captain, he remained virtually in command of the seamen and the ship's operations. At sea, the captain, however superior in social status, was greatly dependent on the master and his team; he could do very little if he came up against the master's active or passive resistance. In practice, captain and master 'ran' the ship together. Their relationship was equivocal. Social superiority went hand in hand with social inferiority. But the division of duties was still fairly well defined as long as the captain regarded himself as a soldier and confined his activities in the main to the command of military operations.

When, under Charles I, gentlemen in growing numbers began to regard themselves not only as soldiers but also as seamen and to treat the master not as a partner but as an inferior and subordinate person, the situation became more tense. The literature of that time bears witness to the increasing friction between captains and masters. Gentlemen captains complained about the arrogance of masters. Masters gibed at the ignorance and incompetence of gentlemen captains; conscious of their vast superiority as the principal sea-experts of the country, they freely expressed their resentment and hostility against these landsmen who tried to arrogate to themselves the master's traditional role as ruler of the ship. Throughout this early phase of their association a captain's impersonal resources of power, as distinct from his personal resources which of course varied from man to man, were not much greater than those of the master. They increased, and the master's position in relation to the captain became correspondingly weaker, ultimately to the extent to which the government's effective control over the seamen increased on the one hand, and the captain's professional efficiency increased on the other.

74

Accordingly, the balance of power between the holders of these posts transformed itself in two fairly distinct stages. After the Restoration, central control over the seamen became more effective without a corresponding increase in the captains' professional efficiency. Thanks to the backing of the court, the gentlemen captains of that period were generally able to enforce the master's obedience and submission; but their position was still far from secure. The power they derived from their superior social position in the country was still counteracted by that which the master derived from his great professional superiority. The master could no longer actively resist the commands of a gentleman captain and show his resentment openly, but he often became indifferent to the needs of the service and showed his resentment in indirect ways. It was still not possible to arrive at a division of functions more or less acceptable to both men and in harmony with the requirements of the service.

Finally, during the first half of the eighteenth century, the professional skill of captains too increased. It was during this period that they were able to assume, not only in name but in fact, complete control of both nautical as well as military operations, and that masters were ultimately relegated to a subordinate position; while retaining some disciplinary functions over sailors, they were in the main confined to the navigation of the ship under the captain's orders. Thus, their professional position was brought into line with their social status; it broadly agreed with that which men of their class usually occupied on land. For while anybody might become a master who had started as a sailor in the merchant service or the navy and who had acquired the highly specialised skill necessary for this post, whether he came from a stock of craftsmen, of yeomen, small traders or workmen, the post and rank of a captain were more and more reserved for men from the gentleman classes, which now included the upper portions of the middle classes. During the second half of the eighteenth century, the captain was, with very few exceptions, the social as well as the professional superior of his master.

His training enabled him as a rule, if not to equal the master in his skill and proficiency as navigator and pilot, at least to supervise his activities effectively. He was, in short, a seaman as well as a gentleman, while the master, though often highly respected on account of his professional qualifications and usually treated as a gentleman, was not a gentleman officer.

In that way, the social standing and the professional functions of captain and master were clearly defined. The scope of action of both men was regulated by a strict and authoritative code. However they varied as individuals, in their official capacity captain and master knew exactly where they stood in relation to each other. Open differences between the two men, therefore, were rare. In most cases, they collaborated smoothly. Their relationship, after more than a century of tensions and struggles, had become stable and unequivocal.

It was even more difficult to arrive at a working solution for the problems arising from the association of master and lieutenant. In its general development, their relationship followed that between master and captain. But from the beginning tensions between the two men were stronger and quarrels more frequent. Lieutenants were usually younger, less powerful and less secure in their position than captains; and even more inferior to masters in sea experience. Masters, on their part, were even less likely to tolerate interference in their work and to take orders from these younger men than they were from the older and socially more experienced captains. And so, from the start, when it became customary for a captain, first in Elizabeth's time and then again more regularly in the time of Charles I, to take with him on board a young gentleman as his lieutenant, frictions and rows between master and lieutenant occurred, as it seems, with great regularity.

Throughout the seventeenth century lieutenants remained mainly military officers. In the daily routine of the ship, they had no specialised functions other than those that came to them as the captain's deputy. But even when during the eighteenth century, as a result of a different training, lieutenants became more proficient in

76

seamanship, the difficulties inherent in a relationship in which the younger and less experience man officially acted as the superior of an older and more experienced never disappeared entirely. Stricter discipline and a clearer demarcation of functions made it easier for both men to adjust themselves to their position and to keep the peace. Many lieutenants and masters were no doubt on the best of terms and collaborated wholeheartedly. Yet so strong was the underlying tendency towards rivalry between what had now become the highest of the warrant officers and the lowest of the commissioned officers that at the beginning of the nineteenth century, after a long period of wars when many lieutenants had finally become expert seamen, some of them began to urge the abolition of masters in the navy on the grounds that lieutenants could do their job just as efficiently. In fact, lieutenants and other commissioned officers, in course of time, took over one after the other of the master's functions until in the end the office of the master disappeared. The uneasy partnership between master and lieutenant ended with the victory of the latter.

THE ROYAL COMMISSIONING POLICY[32]

The struggle for position on board ship between the leading sea-man, the master, and the leading gentlemen, captain and lieutenant, was anything but an isolated event. It was closely connected with the struggle for the commanding positions of the navy between soldiers and sailors. The strife between gentlemen and tarpaulins centred on the question from which of these two groups naval officers should be recruited. This, in turn, was but a sideshow of the general social and political struggles of the seventeenth century. Ultimately, it was the course and outcome of the latter which deter-mined those of the former. The shifting balance of forces in the navy, modified by special conditions and requirements, reflected that in the country at large.

In the navy, the course of these changes was, in broad outline, simple enough: under Henry VIII, and to some extent also under Elizabeth, the seamen (craftsmen), in relation to soldiers (noblemen and gentlemen), gained a fairly strong position. Under the early Stuarts, the gentlemen were in the ascendant. They disappeared from the navy with few exceptions under the Commonwealth; most of the naval officers of that period were professional seamen. Under Charles II and James II the gentlemen again gained the ascendancy over the seamen not so much in term of numbers (we do not know the exact numbers of each group) as in terms of influence and power; they were the favourites of the court; as far as possible the better posts and the more profitable journeys were reserved for them. After 1688, seamen officers again gained ground; for a time, there existed in the navy what appears as an unstable but more equal balance of forces between the two groups. This finally gave way during the eighteenth century to a more stable order of superiority and subordination corresponding to the more stable social and political order of the country as a whole. The dividing line between those who were gentlemen as well as seamen, and those who were seamen but not gentlemen, became more and more pronounced. All the commanding positions were reserved for the former.

Throughout these developments, one can nearly always discern the attempt of those who ruled and administered the navy to find men and other technical means to match the changing requirements of the service and of the country. How far they were able to adjust naval institutions to these requirements and to remedy disparities between means and needs, however, was dependent more often than not on factors beyond their control – factors, seemingly extraneous to the development of a profession, though in fact invariably bound up with it, such as the balance of social forces in the country and sectional interests and status requirements connected with it.

From the beginning when Henry VIII felt it necessary to strengthen his own power, these factors became operative. By all accounts the King and his advisers did exactly what was required at that time. He set the nascent service on the only course from which a navy in the proper sense of the word could emerge. He did not take it for granted, as others after him did, that only noblemen and military gentlemen were fit to plan and to direct military operations at sea as well as on land. Neither by upbringing nor by inclination was he debarred from consulting and employing the only men in the country who knew something about ships and seafaring – professional seamen – although they belonged to the lower orders. And so, largely with their help, he was in fact able to cut loose from the traditional concepts of sea warfare and to adjust the organisation of his military fleet as well as its fighting technique to the specific requirements of the sea.

At the beginning of his reign, the small number of ships at the disposal of the Crown normally carried more soldiers than sailors; at the end, the King owned more than fifty ships, many of them quite powerful, which even in times of war carried more sailors than soldiers. Originally, the direction of military operations at sea was almost exclusively in the hands of military men trained for warfare on land; the military forces on board ship were what they remained in France, in spite of all reforms, up to the French Revolution, an 'army at sea'. Already in 1535, Henry VIII had instructed his admirals that they were not to take any decisions or to embark on any enterprise without calling together their council, which included experienced masters and pilots as well as captains.[33] When he came to the throne, it was the chief aim of military forces at sea to board an enemy ship and to fight there in the same manner in which one fought on land when storming a fortified place. In the course of his reign the technique of sea fighting changed; it became the aim to cripple a hostile vessel by the concentrated fire of heavy guns, to outmanoeuvre it by skilful seamanship and to force it to surrender or to capture it when its crew was already decimated. It was a technique which only experienced seamen could use successfully.

79

Perfected by Elizabethan seamen, it later helped to foil the attempted invasion of 1588, and it became, still further developed, the characteristic fighting technique of the English navy under the Commonwealth, again at a time when the professional seaman were given a large share in the planning and direction of naval affairs.

All these changes were due, no doubt, in great measure to the King's good sense and his insight into the requirements of a military fleet. But he would hardly have been able to put his insight into practice had not the measures demanded by it agreed with his general policy towards different social groups, dictated by his needs for maintaining his power by keeping the balance of social and political forces in the country. Briefly speaking, the power of the old nobility which regarded the command of military operations as its traditional preserve was on the decline. Yet its members still represented a greater threat to the King's power than opponents from any other class. To counterbalance their influence the King frequently used as his helpers men of inferior social status. He had no scruples about appointing persons of common descent like Cromwell or Cranmer to the highest offices in his kingdom. Nor did he hesitate to let his nobles know what his policy was when they protested. The King's Privy Council on one of these occasions wrote:

> If it please his Majesty, to appoint the meanest men . . . to rule and govern in that place, is not his Graces auctoritie sufficient to cause all men to serve his Grace under him without respect of the very estate of that personage?

And the King himself added:

> Surely we woll not be bounde of a necessitie to be served there with lordes. But we wolbe served with such men what degree soever they be as we shall appointe to the same . . .[34]

80

The same policy applied to the military forces at sea, and the relatively strong position which the seamen obtained in the King's fleet as a result was one of the main conditions, if not the main condition, for the relatively early and speedy transformation of England's 'army by sea' into a navy proper. Naval developments, in all likelihood, would have taken a different turn, had, at that time, the nobility with its old tradition of military leadership still been firmly entrenched in power. For wherever that was the case, land-soldiers ruled on board ship; seamen were confined to their traditional role as providers of transport; the organisation of the fighting fleet was modelled on that of the army, and sea warfare on land warfare.

A SHIFT IN THE CENTRE OF GRAVITY

This interdependence between the country's general social and political order and the character of its naval forces is brought out most strikingly if one compares the conditions of the navy under Henry VIII with those under Charles I. In the reign of King Charles, the King's fleet returned to the state in which it had been prior to Henry VIII's reforms. In its organisation and its fighting technique, it began to show features characteristic more of an 'army by sea' or perhaps an *armée navale* in the French sense – rather than of a navy in the English sense. Thus at a time when England's political system was beginning to show strong tendencies towards developing on the same lines as continental monarchies, especially that of France, England's navy began to assume some of the characteristics of continental navies. Most of the commanding positions were given to noblemen and gentlemen whose training was, at best, that of soldiers. They planned the operations and ruled on board ship. In the main, seamen were confined to their task of conducting soldiers overseas. One could not do entirely without officers and naval administrators of the 'common sort' who were expert seamen; but

81

as far as possible they and the seamen generally were relegated to an inferior position.

Boteler, who was himself a man of quality and a soldier with some sea experience probably expressed the general opinion of his circles when he wrote in his *Naval Dialogues*:

ADMIRAL: We have formerly consented in this, that the nobility are by all means to be encouraged to the sea services; and that the chief Officers of the Navy, and those of the Council of War, are to be of noble birth and education; and does not this hold as well in all the other Captains?

CAPTAIN: Truly yes. And that not only for the better breeding of our nobility ... in general, in this kind of service, which so much concerns us; but also in regard to that free and frequent access and converse, which in all actions of war is requirable and unavoidable betwixt the General himself and the Captains; and for which the mere bred seamen are generally very ill provided; and besides it may probably, and with reason, be expected (in regard of their very blood and birth) that the touch of honour and reputation should work more actively upon them, than with the right-down mariners, and mere sea-bred man, [be he otherwise, in point of sufficiency for his trade, never so practic and sufficient].[35]

The antagonism between the two groups became more pronounced. People became more conscious of the fact that the navy had among its officers not only individuals of different social standing, but two different groups – gentlemen commanders and commanders 'bred to the sea'. Each group had its partisans in the country, and its standard arguments. The gentlemen maintained that 'mere sea bred men' lacked the military experience and the sense of honour required of military leaders. The seamen pointed to the obvious professional incompetence of most of the gentlemen who were sent down from the court to rule over them on board ship.

The King himself, it seems, was hardly aware of this controversy; most probably he was not aware of it. Unperturbed, he
pursued his policy of appointing as many courtiers as he found
willing to go to the commanding positions of his fleet. He tried to
induce young men of quality to go to the sea as volunteers and
lieutenants of the navy. At the same time, knowing little of the true
feelings of the seamen, he tried to keep them contented and hoped to
win their loyalty by raising their wages and improving, to a certain
degree, their general conditions.

As it turned out, he had good reasons for this policy. Like that of
his predecessors, it was largely dictated by the general conditions of
his power and well in line with his general policy in the country. For
since Henry VIII's time the balance of forces in the country had
changed. The struggle of the nobles for the preservation of their
feudal independence and privileges had come to an end. The power
of the central authorities personified by the King had outgrown that
of any coalition of noblemen. But within the framework of the more
centralised state there had gradually grown up an aristocratic society,
composed partly of old and partly of new elements a new upper class
formation, with the court as its centre, and ramifications throughout
the country.[36] Its members were fairly uniform in their standards
and ideals and their whole way of life. And it was mainly from this
court society that the King selected the men on whom he relied for
the preservation and extension of his power and whom he entrusted
with the key positions in his realm, including the highest offices in
the state and the command of the armed forces.

For while in Henry VIII's time the nobles had still been,
potentially, the strongest force from which the King could expect
opposition, in King Charles's time the centre of gravity had shifted
to other sections of the population. Many noblemen still feared the
King's attempts at establishing his personal rule. But many others,
especially those connected with the court, regarded the King's cause
as their own. The Lords were divided. They were no longer in a

position to resist the King's bid for unlimited power without the help of the Commons. With the country's increasing dependence on trade the political and social weight of urban groups organised in boroughs and corporations had steadily grown. Puritanism, spreading among them since Tudor times, had given them greater cohesion and an increased uniformity of outlook. It was well on its way towards becoming their common way of life – a way of life no less pronounced than, but radically different from, that of the courtiers. They, and above all the City of London together with groups of country gentlemen, now formed through their representatives in the Commons the spearhead of the opposition which limited the King's scope of action and prevented him from playing the part which he thought was his due.

The attitude of the King towards the two groups represented in the navy reflected the alignment of forces in the country. In spite of their professional shortcomings, he persisted in appointing courtiers as lieutenants, captains and flag officers in preference to professional seamen not only because he himself was by upbringing a courtier, but because he knew that in the country's internal struggle they were on his side while the seamen, fluctuating and often inarticulate as their political sympathies were, had close links with the groups which, as he saw it, denied him his right as King. In fact, he was so confident of the success of this policy that at the beginning of the civil war when parliament tried to gain control of the navy, he himself for months did very little to counter their activities, thinking that there was no need for it because, as Clarendon reports, he had many gentlemen settled in the command of his ships of whose affection and fidelity His Majesty was assured 'that they would at all times repair to his service whenever he require it'. And it was not the fault of these gentlemen officers themselves that his policy failed.[37]

The choice of naval officers, in other words, was determined by considerations which in modern times often escape attention. In the seventeenth century, in England, where the country's representatives denied their rulers the means for maintaining a standing army in times of peace, the navy played the same double role which armies played in most continental countries, though not quite to the same extent: it could be used as a weapon against internal as well as external enemies of the King.

3

The Development of the Midshipman

In the seventeenth century boys from all classes entered the navy in the traditional manner, under the patronage of a captain as his followers or servants. These boys were called volunteers, in contra-distinction probably to other members of the crew, many of whom had been pressed into the service. After some less successful attempts in the seventeenth century, in the eighteenth a distinction gradually came to be made more permanently and consistently between different kinds of volunteers. Boys between the ages of 11 and 14 who came from a gentlemanly background and whose family had some influence with the captain were kept apart from the other sea-boys under various names: first as 'volunteers by order', then as 'volunteers of the first class' or sometimes as 'gentleman volunteers'.[1] They formed a separate establishment.

These first-class volunteers had certain special privileges to mark their status as young gentlemen and future naval officers. They were for instance allowed to walk the quarterdeck, to wear naval uniform and to hire a servant if they had enough money. On the larger ships they often had a schoolmaster. Sometimes the chaplain took a hand in their education or, if he was so inclined, the captain himself. In that way they might complete their education and learn some of the things which it was thought necessary for a gentleman to know, including perhaps fencing and dancing, though a good deal more was probably learned from life than from lessons.

86

At the same time they were put in the charge of an experienced seaman who catered for them, looked after their clothes and their mess and generally acted as their tutor and supervisor. And by him they were taught to knot and to reef or to send down yard and mast by themselves. In short they were given a kind of cockpit education and trained in a practical manner more or less like seamen apprentices.

This was, or was supposed to be, the first step of a young gentleman on his way to the commissioned ranks. In practice, of course, many naval officers never went through this training. Friendly captains kept their name on the ship's books to comply with regulations while they themselves continued to live with their parents.

The second and more important step was the appointment as midshipman. As a rule captains did not promote their young charges to that post before they were 15. As midshipmen they completed their training both as seamen and military officers. On the one hand they were now 'oldsters' and behaved not unlike the older college boys of their time. They traditionally frightened the 'youngsters', the first-class volunteers, with time-honoured tales of dead men dangling from the yards or of Flemish horses to be found aloft. They had time and inclination to do a lot of mischief and played all kinds of practical jokes, so we learn of masters walking around their ship with a piece of strong leather in their pocket for the young gentlemen if they got out of hand.

They sweated over their logarithms;[2] they caroused.[3] And, if one can trust W. Falconer, who wrote the poem 'The Midshipman' and who was once well known as author of the *Universal Dictionary of the Marine*, their cabins themselves showed their hybrid character as both gentlemen and seaman:

> Chesterfield's page polite, *The Seaman's Guide*,
> An half-eat biscuit, Congreve's *Mourning Bride*,
> Bestrewed with powder, in confusion lie.

On the other hand, there were duties to perform:

> Hark! younder voice in hollow murmur swells:
> Hark! younder voice the Mid to Duty calls?
> Thus summoned by the Gods, he deigns to go.
> But first makes known his Consequence below:
> At Slavery rails, scorns lawless Sway to Hell,
> And damns the power allowed a whit lapel:
> Vows that he's free: – to stoop, to cringe disdains –
> Ascends the Ladder and resumes his Chains.[4]

These duties were by no means inconsiderable. He might be stationed in one of the tops, or put to watch, or perhaps put in charge of a prize. He had to 'second the orders of the lieutenant and other officers'.[5] One can say that the duties and the status of midshipmen fluctuated to some extent between those of a naval cadet and a junior officer. And, of course, they all hoped, after two years as midshipmen and after passing an often rather perfunctory examination by the captain, to procure for themselves a commission as naval lieutenant.

Thus during the eighteenth century the place of a midshipman became definitely the most important stepping-stone for a young gentleman who wished to become a naval officer. In fact it became the lynchpin of the whole system which enabled naval officers to fulfil their double functions as seamen and military gentlemen. Together with that of first-class volunteers, it satisfied both the professional requirements of the naval service for a training establishment where young gentlemen could gain some experience in seamanship, and the status requirements of naval officers and prospects of parents of naval officers who demanded a separate training establishment for young gentlemen maintaining the normal social distinctions between gentlemen and the lower classes.

It was in fact a rather ingenious compromise between conflicting tendencies which had struggled in the navy for more than a

88

century. But this happy solution of a long drawn out struggle was by no means due primarily to the inspiration of a few intelligent members of the Admiralty or the naval administration. In fact, during the eighteenth century, regulations from above were still at least as much guided by practices and usages which developed by trial and error directly on board the ships as they were guiding them. Recruitment and selection of future naval officers were still for the greater part in the hands of captains and flag officers. And traditions established among the captains, modified of course by their personal inclinations, largely determined how young volunteers and midshipmen were trained or whether they were trained at all. For the greater part of the eighteenth century all that the official regulations required of the future naval officer was that he should have been for six years at sea with one of his Majesty's ships, that he should have served for two of these six years as midshipman and that he should have been passed by his captain before he could be given a commission as lieutenant by the Admiralty or, in special cases, by an admiral.

Yet, even after this training scheme combining a seaman's training with that of a military officer and gentleman had been more or less firmly established in the navy, like many another compromise it did not always work smoothly. In fact, the question of whether the training and duties of seamen were really compatible with those of military gentlemen never ceased to be a serious topic for discussions among naval officers as long as the navy remained the fleet of sailing ships, although in the eighteenth and nineteenth centuries it was no longer – as it had appeared to be in the seventeenth – an almost insoluble problem.

During the first half of the eighteenth century it was still partly a controversy between two different groups of naval officers, as it had been throughout the seventeenth, and not alone a controversy concerning the professional training, functions and status of naval officers. Thus in November 1755 Captain Edward Thompson, then a lieutenant and later well known among naval officers as the author of many celebrated sea-songs, wrote in a letter:

> We are likewise to recollect that all commanders of men of war are not gentlemen nor men of education – I know a great part are brave men, but much greater seamen. I allow the maxim of learning to obey, before we command ourselves; but still there is no reason to be vulgar . . . tho' there is already such a reformation in the British navy, as would even remove those satyrical epithets so generally made use of to their disrepute. The last war, a chaw of tobacco, a ratan, and a rope of oaths, were sufficient qualifications to constitute a lieutenant; but now education and good manners are the study of all; and so far from effeminacy, that I am of the opinion the present race of officers will as much eclipse the veterans of 1692, as the polite the vulgar.[6]

At that time, the naval profession was still struggling to establish itself in the eyes of the world as a gentleman's profession and to find the right balance between seamanship on the one hand and the knowledge and standards of behaviour of military officers and gentlemen on the other.[7] There were obviously still quite a number of officers in the navy who had started as sea-boys, had become in course of time masters of merchantmen or of men-of-war, and from there as it quite normally happened in the seventeenth century had passed into the commissioned ranks. The fairly widespread opposition of this period to 'too much seamanship' was still closely connected with an opposition to 'too many seaman-officers'.[8] Early in the nineteenth century, on the other hand, during the last period of the sailing navy, the pendulum had swung far in the opposite direction.

Prior to this time, during the sixteenth and seventeenth centuries, the institutional scaffolding of a naval officer's training and career provided by government regulations was even more scanty. In fact, one might easily be deceived if one were to look upon government orders or the ideas of kings or naval administrators as the principal driving forces in the development of the English naval profession, or for that matter as the main sources of its history. These regulations and ideas frequently show the practical problems and the difficulties confronting naval administrators and naval officers of that period. But in many cases these difficulties seem to persist in spite of repeated orders and regulations from above. While all over Europe the power of kings and princes to regulate the lives of their subjects according to their ideas increased and asserted itself, in England, the institutions of that period – the naval profession among them – grew into shape through the interplay of a number of forces of which the court was only one. Governmental regulations certainly determined to a larger or smaller extent the practices and relationships in the navy itself. But these on their part had a weight of their own. Their development often led to a change of regulations. The growth of the English naval profession, therefore, took the form of a slow, but fairly continuous sequence of changes with many ups and downs. And this type of development had considerable influence on the specific character of the English naval profession. One need only compare it with corresponding developments on the continent and particularly in France, in order to see its singularity and its significance.

4

Achieving Maritime Supremacy

THE ATLANTIC RIVALRY

Paradoxically enough, the conflicts and quarrels between the nobles and the gentlemen on the one hand and the mariners from common descent on the other were not only the prelude to the fusion of gentlemen and seamen into a hierarchically organised team but one of the means by which this fusion was brought about. Some of the most characteristic features of the English navy and the establishment of English naval officers may be ascribed to the fact that these dissensions were not simply brushed aside and driven underground by an order planned and enforced from above. It contributed greatly towards amalgamating some of the qualities and experiences of both groups that they were left a certain initiative and some scope for working out among themselves – bitterly quarrelling at times, collaborating at others and often doing both at the same time – a *modus vivendi*, however precarious.

We need only glance over to France in order to see the difference. Partly on account of her military entanglements on the continent, partly for other reasons, France entered the Atlantic rivalry later than England. She actively took part in it on fairly equal terms only at the end of the seventeenth century. Yet the initial problem was the same. The military gentlemen were no seamen, apart from those few who had served as officers in the Mediterranean fleet of galleys. The professional mariners, on the other hand, familiar with the handling of sailing ships, were not very willing to submit to the command of landsmen and military discipline. In fact, it can be said that the same problem and the same difficulties are to be found in the history of every country passing through the same stage of development. The antagonism between military gentlemen and professional seamen with all it involved is one of those constitutional social problems arising wherever a sailing fleet differentiates into a specialised military and a specialised mercantile branch, and related problems appear even in the evolution of galley fleets. Yet, the way these problems are solved and the solution itself varies according to the political and social structure of every country. Only a comparative sociological investigation of several countries could bring to light more fully this interdependency between the structure and character of a country as a whole and those of her navy. It was for example characteristic of France, as of every other great military power under the rule of an absolute prince, that the social superiority and the caste-like exclusiveness of the hereditary military class, the *noblesse d'épée*, was comparatively great; correspondingly high was the social barrier between this upper class and the middle class of craftsmen and artisans to which the leading seamen belonged. If nothing else, this fact alone would have prevented the antagonism between gentlemen and seamen from taking, for any length of time, the form of an open feud as it did in England. In Spain this exclusiveness of the military class, its contempt for the seaman and his work were even greater. These differences in structure and attitude – seen from a certain distance perhaps no more than differences of degree – led to corresponding differences in the development and the structure of the three naval establishments and of the naval profession. The greater superiority and exclusiveness of the military class was reflected in the barrier between gentlemen officers and craftsmen officers on board the ships and in the channels provided for the rise of the latter in the ranks. Generally speaking one could say these barriers were higher and more rigid in France than in England and higher in Spain

93

than in France; these channels in France wider and more numerous than in Spain, and in England, as we shall see, wider than in both these countries. Moreover, these attitudes of the gentlemen towards the seamen were also reflected in their attitudes towards seamanship; in that way they affected not only the standards and traditions of naval officers in the three countries but also the general conduct of the three navies. The fewer contacts there were between military gentlemen and professional seamen, the more did the former preserve the character of military men, and the less did they acquire the character and master the art of a seaman. In fact, it was only in England that the gentlemen, after the long feud with the seamen, submitted in the end to a seaman's training. In England alone, therefore, the standards set for a naval officer gradually attained a fair measure of equilibrium between seamanship and military virtues. The symbol of this amalgamation of qualities formerly more or less peculiar to different social groups was the rank of a midshipman, the station through which, from the first quarter of the eighteenth century onwards, a young gentleman had to pass on his way to the commission ranks of the navy. In this station he had to learn and to perform with his own hands a good many of the duties of an ordinary seaman. No similar station and no similar training existed in either the French or the Spanish navy of that time. In France, as in Spain, the preparation of a young gentleman for his future career as a naval officer was mainly military in character. It was enacted in 1686 that he had to spend a short time on board a ship, not as a sailor but as a soldier. As for seamanship he was taught it very thoroughly on land and he had to prove in an examination that he was conversant with the theory of navigation and the use of nautical instruments. Everything was well regulated and well organised, as befitted the country of an absolute prince. The French naval officers were, in fact, generally reputed to be better mathematicians than the English, and more experienced in the theory of naval tactics and strategy. Yet they were equally reputed to be inferior to the English in practical

94

seamanship, and there were many encounters between the two navies to prove it. One could find, during the *ancien régime*, a few excellent seamen among the higher officers of the French navy, men like Duguay-Trouin who had started as a *corsaire* at the end of the seventeenth century and De Guichen in the middle of the eighteenth century, but among French naval officers they were an exception rather than the rule. In a continental country like France, the social weight and the prestige of the land army with its strict social barriers between noblemen and gentlemen who apart from fighting never did any manual work, and the lower orders who did manual work, were far too great for people in the military service at sea to attempt or to desire an adaptation to the special conditions at sea. To a considerable extent throughout the *ancien régime* the land army always set the pattern after which the sea-army was modelled. Every deviation, an innovation like that associated with the position of a midshipman – putting a gentlemen, temporarily, almost on the same level as a seamen – would necessarily have lowered the prestige of the whole class of naval officers. In that regard nothing can be more characteristic of the difference between the old French and the old English navy than the name of the former. It was called *l'armée navale*.

It is this wider context from which we have to view the development and the characteristics of England's naval profession. Following the narrow track of national history alone we can neither get a clear picture of the structural features and the driving forces common to all the military fleets of the great European powers and to their officers, nor of those special conditions which worked towards the making of England's navy and the English naval profession; and though not much room can be given here to the study of other than the English navy, a few comparative observations may help to bring into fuller relief the basic differences. One of these, and the cause of many others, was the rigid social barrier maintained, for a long time, between what was originally the fleet arm of the land army, between the military officers on the one hand and the seamen on the other in

95

the military fleet of both France and Spain. In a short tract on 'The ill management of the Spanish ships' probably written at the beginning of the seventeenth century, Sir William Monson wrote:

> Notwithstanding the necessity they have of sailors there is no nation less respectful of them than the Spaniards, which is the principal cause of their want of them; and till Spain alters this course let them never think to be well served at sea. The meanest soldier will not stick to tyrannise over the poor sailors, like a master over his spaniel, and shall be countenanced in it by his land commander ... Our discipline is far different, and indeed quite contrary ... He [the captain] sees no injury shall be offered the sailors by the soldiers, but carries himself indifferently betwixt both.[1]

The master mariners, the seaman-officers on Spanish ships, were completely subordinate to the military officers, and the two classes did not mix; consequently they did not learn from each other. It would be quite wrong to assume, of course, that this social barrier between the two groups did not exist in England or was ever broken down. All one can say is in fact that it was less high and more elastic than in Spain or in France. As in many other cases, this pattern of social relationships determined the pattern of behaviour. The naval officers of France and Spain kept on behaving more like military officers of the land army and less like seamen than the English naval officers. To quote a comparative observation from a much later period, Sarrazin, field marshal of the French king, wrote in 1816:

> Les marins anglais nous sont supérieurs, non par leur courage ni par leur patriotisme, mais par leur expérience qui est la pratique de la théorie ... Un capitaine anglais est presque toujours le meilleur matelot de son bord; il n'y a pas de manœuvre qu'il ne soit à même de commander et d'exécuter. Souvent on le voit mettre la main à l'ouvrage avec un zèle qu'on louerait dans un aspirant ... Osons le dire, le contraire

existe à bord de nos vaisseaux. Quand un de nos officiers supérieurs
arrive sur le pont il se croit méprisé et il prend un air boudeur . . .²

[It is not by their courage or their patriotism that the English naval
personnel is superior to ours, but they have more experience which
means more practice to their theory. . . . An English captain is nearly
always the best seaman on board ship. Every manoeuvre he orders he
can execute himself. Often enough one can see him lending a hand with
the work with an energy that would earn praise for a young volunteer . . .
Let us say frankly the opposite is the case on our own ships. If a French
officer takes up his station on board ship he believes himself despised
and assumes a supercilious air . . .]³

This was perhaps a slightly idealised picture of the average
English naval officer of the Napoleonic war coming as it did from the
pen of a French Royalist who was anxious to explain to his vanquished fellow countrymen the reasons for their inferiority at sea.
There can be no doubt, however, that the English naval officers were
better seamen than the French.

At first glance the comparatively high level of seamanship in the
old British navy may appear simply as the natural consequence of
Britain's insular position. However, it is only if we translate the
geographical position into human terms and see how it influenced
Britain's social and political development that we can uncover the
links between the two. Skilled seamen were bred along the shores of
France as along those of the British Isles. Since, however, the lead in
military actions was usually in the hands not of seamen but of
noblemen and gentlemen, the level of seamanship in the specialised
military fleet in all these countries was dependent on the extent to
which these military officers of upper-class extraction adapted themselves to what was originally the art of a lower class. That in England,
after a long struggle, these classes adapted themselves better to the
special conditions of a military service at sea than in most continental

97

countries was, in part, undoubtedly due to the fact that on an island the social value of a land army was not as great as on the continent, and less great, therefore, was the social weight and the prestige attached to the military character of a man – military in the sense of the land army. In that way, Britain's insular position was certainly an important factor in her social development in general and, more especially, in that of her naval profession. Yet the example of Holland suggests that it was less indispensable a factor than it may seem. For different reasons, Holland's strength and greatness too was not centred in its army to the same extent as that of almost all the other continental countries which counted in the power game of the seventeenth century. There, too, the military character of its nobility was less outspoken, the social barrier separating the upper classes from the various middle classes and, correspondingly, the military officers from the seaman-officers less rigid and immovable, and the standard of seamanship of her military fleet equally high.

DEVELOPMENTS IN SPAIN

To what extent the development of such a fleet and the professional character of its officers were dependent on the social and political development of a country as a whole is perhaps nowhere shown more clearly than in the history of Spain. It may be debatable whether or not the physical conditions of this country, its climate, its geographical position, the soil and its products were less favourable to the development of both the commercial and the fighting fleet. About the grave impediments placed in its way by Spain's social and political conditions there can be no doubt. The low social status of seamen, and the contempt in which they were held, were part of a general attitude towards manual work. It was, in part, a legacy of the age-long struggle between Spaniards and Moors. The victorious Spaniards left all the menial work to the vanquished, whether slaves or not. This association with a subject population, in the course of time, made manual work generally contemptible beyond what it was in other countries. That noblemen and gentlemen could not work with their hands without losing caste was the accepted rule all over Europe and, for all we know, outside Europe as well. But in Spain this rule applied to all freeborn Spaniards; even the poorer classes tried to live like gentlemen. Pepys, passing through Spain in 1683, wrote in his diary:

> I saw their pretence to gentility, among the poorest people and a declaration that a blow is not to be given to a white man (as they call themselves) spoils all authority. And so I see it is in private families, all are equal, and their civility to beggars and being equal in the churches, in their places of devotion etc. helps all towards it.[4]

To Pepys, the expression 'white man' with all it implied was at that time evidently something quite new. Spain was, in fact, the first of the Western countries with a race problem of its own. The ruling Spaniards expressed their own social superiority first over the Moors at home, and later over their colonial subjects, not only in terms of religion but also in terms of colour. After part of the subject population had become converted to Christianity, religion alone could no longer serve as a distinguishing mark and a rallying point for the master race. The necessity, moreover, for maintaining the distinction between those who belonged to the ruling people (often a small minority) and the subject population produced a strong feeling of solidarity among the former. The code of behaviour, the scale of social values set up by the proud and militant Spanish nobility, permeated gradually the whole of the white population. A freeborn Spaniard, even if he was poor, asked to be respected as a white gentleman. Spain was also the first of the modern nations beset with that affliction known to students of modern society as the problem of the poor whites. The fear of losing caste, of falling down

99

to the level of the subject races, debarred many Spaniards from taking up those professions which in other countries provided a living for the poorer classes. On the other hand those Spaniards who were engaged in one of the lower occupations, many of them probably of mixed descent, were treated with contempt, sometimes almost like outcasts. According to the scale of values, even begging was less contemptible and degrading; and there were, in fact, a good many Spaniards too proud to work with their own hands who lived on the crumbs from the table of their better-placed compatriots, waiting for the time when they might again show their valour in battle. And these attitudes, bent on maintaining the domination of the ruling population over the lower orders throughout the Empire, were fostered not only by Spanish society but by the whole might of Spain's absolutist state, which made them all the more rigid.

These social and political conditions were among the chief causes that debarred Spain from becoming a great manufacturing country, as they prevented her from becoming a great seafaring power. We need not here go into the wider problem of Spain's economic development. No doubt it had a great bearing on the development of her military fleet. However, Spain's inability to follow up her conquest of a vast and rich empire with a corresponding development of her trading and manufacturing capacities was not, as it is sometimes supposed, the actual cause for the backwardness of her military fleet. Both these deficiencies can be traced back to the same sources. The very qualities and conditions which made her, for a time, the greatest military power on earth prevented her from becoming a great commercial power and a great sea power.

As for the naval profession, it is only too obvious how these conditions affected its development. The strict exclusiveness of all the people who regarded themselves and wished to be regarded as pure Spaniards – [an exclusiveness] acquired by their domination over a Moorish population, further strengthened by the rule of a relatively small Spanish community over a vast empire – subsisted inside Spain, as it did in some parts of her empire, long after the subject population had become partly assimilated and ceased to be a danger to the ruling people. Changing gradually from what we might call a purely racial into a social attitude, it was directed against all those performing lower-class work whether they were of Moorish descent or not. It was part of this general attitude when, 'on board the Spanish ships the sailors were flouted and despised as a troublesome necessity for navigation', as people 'who occupied space that, otherwise, would have been available for soldiers, [and] who, whenever possible were sacrificed to the comfort of the soldiers, humiliated and degraded in their own estimation'.[5] The military service of the King, the army and its officers – the core of the Spanish empire – was, naturally, among the professions which ranked highest in the social hierarchy of Spain. The profession of a seaman ranked among those low-class occupations not fit for a pure Spaniard, whether rich or poor, noble or non-noble. The gulf between the two groups was unbridgeable. In fact, it needs a glance over to these great military countries on the continent in order to see how singular were the conditions which, in England, led to a certain amalgamation between some of the qualities and duties of these two social groups, and thereby to the emergence of a specialised naval profession. In Spain, there was no way open for such an amalgamation. The descent from the social level of a military man to that of a seaman was too steep, the loss of prestige involved too great.

Much has been said about the natural, almost congenital inaptitude of the Spaniard for the sea. Whether this inaptitude was really inborn, a racial characteristic of the Spanish community, is hard to say. The historic reasons, in any case, are plain enough. A profession held in low esteem does not stimulate perfection or encourage improvements; nor does it attract the most able and ambitious people. Yielding little respect and social power for those engaged in it, there is little hope that it will ever flourish – especially under a rigid social and political system like that of Spain, holding out scant prospect of a change. It seems to be generally true not only that in all the continental countries with a great military tradition the army overshadowed the military fleet by its greater power and prestige, which is almost self-evident, but also that the lower prestige of the naval force proved in many ways an obstacle to its development. Quite apart from the fact that in all these countries the land force attracted the better sort of people, it also more or less hampered both the administration and the officers from evolving for the fighting fleet institutional and professional models of its own – that is to say, from moulding it into a 'Navy' in the English sense of the word. Spain, on account of the rigidity of her social institutions and standards, went to the extreme in this direction. The excessive social weight of her aristocracy with its great military tradition stifled the autonomous development of her military fleet. In a way, the navy remained a mere dependency of the army. Consequently, in 1805 we find it just as inefficient and its officers as much lacking in seamanship as in 1588.[6]

One might, of course, say that mere reasoning could have taught the Spanish people and its rulers that they could only hope to maintain their rule over their overseas dominions by developing into a great sea power and by building up an efficient fighting fleet. Yet if there is one thing to be learnt from the history of Spain, it is the persistence, one might almost say the obduracy, with which attitudes and social standards are reproduced long after they have ceased to be useful and even if they prove obnoxious – provided that, traditionally, a high social prestige is attached to them and that they are deemed essential for the maintenance of an existing social order. For those brought up with these attitudes and standards, they usually represent a barrier which their thoughts can never surmount. They cannot be broken down by mere reasoning; they can only be altered together with the social system to which the prestige and the power they yield are due. The attitudes, the scale of social values evolved by Spain's militant nobility in the heyday of their domination over inferior

races and gradually accepted by part of the Spanish people generally, in the long run proved obnoxious for both Spain's commercial
and maritime development. It was in accordance with these standards
that the transport of goods from the colonies to Spain was organised
as a royal monopoly, breaking the initiative of the Spanish merchants.
According to this scale of values the seamen, like other artisans, were
kept in a low and humiliating position. As for Spain's navy, of course,
many attempts were made to improve its conditions and especially
its standard of seamanship, but the remedies chosen – whatever they
were, schools for seamen or a better theoretical training of officers –
never touched the root of the matter. They never attacked those
social standards which forbade a military officer any closer contact
with the seamen and their work. It was evidently beyond the power
even of an absolute prince to force upon his officers training and
duties which they themselves would have regarded as a social degra-
dation. However, nothing was further from the mind of those who
ruled Spain than to lower the prestige of Spain's military men, or to
break down some of the barriers separating noblemen and gentlemen
from the inferior classes. If anything, absolutism tended to stiffen
these barriers. For it was to a large extent upon the social divisions
among his own people that the rule of an absolute monarch rested.[7]

DEVELOPMENTS IN FRANCE

In that regard French absolutism showed itself no less strict than
that of Spain. Colbert's famous *Code des armées navales*, published
in 1689, the basic regulation for France's naval force, laid it down – in
accordance with the standards set by the land army and certainly
with the intentions of Louis XIV himself – that the commissioned
ranks of the naval army were open only to noblemen.[8] A few years
before, in 1682, Louis XIV had created – or actually revived, for a
similar attempt in 1678 had failed – special military formations

called 'Gardes-marines', from which the officers of the naval army had to be selected and where they were trained. The aim of this institution was similar to that assumed in the English naval force during the eighteenth century by the station of midshipman on board the ships. But the rank of midshipman – as we have seen, originally a stage in the career of a professional seaman – assumed its special character by amalgamating these seaman's duties with others proper for a gentleman of the fighting profession. The Garde-marine was purely military in character, with an additional theoretical training in navigation and nautical strategy, thereby embodying the strict dividing line between gentlemen and those who did manual labour. It was expressly stated that only noblemen were to be admitted into the Gardes-marines and, before being admitted, candidates had to produce a certificate proving their descent from the *noblesse d'épée*.[9] A little later a concession was made to families *d'honnête condition et vivant noblement* – that is to say, living on the income of their estate and not connected with commerce, trade or any of the lower occupations. Their sons could also be admitted into the Gardes-marines.

Colbert, himself a member of the highest class of bourgeois and not too great a friend of the hereditary nobility, was by no means blind to the advantages to be derived from an infusion of professional seamen into the corps of naval officers. It was due to him that a few seamen who had distinguished themselves, mainly as privateers – people like Duguay-Trouin[10] or Jean Bart[11] – got a commission in the navy; and, as the command of smaller war vessels like sloops and frigates were not particularly in request by noblemen and gentlemen, he made sure that it could be given to seamen. However, the forces on the other side were too strong. Even these few concessions aroused the wrath of the military nobility. Another strict dividing line was established between those ranks open to people of lower social status and those reserved for noblemen and gentlemen. The one were called officers of the *petit état*, the others officers of the *grand état.* The two groups did not mix, and there was no way open from the station of the former into the ranks of the latter.

The social tension between noblemen and gentlemen on the one hand, and those who came from the bourgeois middle classes on the other, made itself felt in the naval history of France as in that of England. But in France it found its expression not in a long and open feud between the military officers and the seaman-officers. Within the social hierarchy of absolutist France the seaman-officers and the whole social group of craftsmen and tradesmen or perhaps even merchants to which they belonged ranked far too low; they were far too inferior in social status and power for an open and active resistance against the military officers. It was the civil administration of the French navy, the *corps de la plume*, which battled constantly with the hierarchy of military naval officers, the *corps de l'épée*, striving hotly and quite successfully for the strengthening of its own control over naval affairs and to limit that of the military men. This dual control of the French navy by two rival corps was started at the time of Louis XIV; it lasted throughout the *ancien régime*. It accounted for a good many of the differences that we find not only in the conduct of the French and the English navy but also in the whole structure of the naval establishment, in the order and hierarchy of naval offices in the two countries. It was for instance due to this different alignment of social forces that on French ships the *écrivain* or scrivener, the equivalent of a purser, was, as member of the *corps de plume*, a far more important man than his English counterpart and actually stood higher in the hierarchy of naval offices. The political commissar of the Revolution was but a modified replica of the civil commissary, who as a representative of the civil administration supervised the conduct of the officers on board the ship. Generally, one can say that nothing perhaps shows more strikingly the extent to which the genesis and the formation of a naval establishment was dependent on the social and political structure of a country as a whole than these differences between the English and the French navy. It was the basic principle of French absolutism – and, with many variations, of that of absolutism generally – to divide the administration of the country, socially, into two compartments, one reserved for noblemen, the other for people of bourgeois extraction. Louis XIV had brought this system almost to perfection; it was among the chief sources of his power. He saw to it that the division and rivalry as well as the equilibrium between the two groups were rigorously maintained.[12] He allocated all the higher offices of the civil administration to the highest class of bourgeois, the *noblesse de robe*. The rule was slightly – but only slightly – relaxed during the eighteenth century. Under Louis XIV himself, no nobleman, that is to say no member of the *noblesse d'épée*, was ever appointed to the office of minister or to any other inferior office of the French administration. On the other hand all the court offices, all the higher military, and most of the diplomatic appointments were reserved for the hereditary nobility.

Between 1670 and 1689, in his various attempts to reorganise his fighting forces at sea he acted on exactly the same principle. He created two distinct powers, *deux pouvoirs distincts* as a French historian said, one civil, the other military, delimiting the duties and responsibilities of each group 'avec une rigoureuse exactitude dans le code de 1689, afin d'arrêter toute extension d'autorité soit de la part de l'élément militaire sur les fonctions civiles, soit de la part de l'administration sur le corps des officiers' [laid down with such a rigorous exactness in the 1689 Code to prevent any shift of authority either on the part of the military to encroach upon civil functions or on the part of the civil authorities to encroach upon matters solely concerning the officers corps].[13] As a blueprint, this *ordonnance* of 1689 is a magnificent example for the lucid and methodical spirit of French absolutism. Compared with this French *Code des armées navales*, all the attempts to improve the organisation of the English navy made during the same period by people like Pepys, the Duke of York, and the naval administration of William and Mary, appear as half-measures. Even had they desired to resort to more radical measures to do more, these English statesmen simply did not have the power to do so. They had to reckon with those groups or persons who, rightly or wrongly, might feel that their interests were threatened by a wholesale reorganisation. The power afforded to some of these groups by the political system of England was, of course, far greater than in France. Consequently the French naval force became, for a time, a most efficient weapon and a formidable threat to its competitors, judged at least from the outside. Already in 1684 Pepys had noted, a little enviously it seems, 'I have had much information given me of the order among the French beyond ours, doing their business with more command, more obedience, more silence, all at once, the working of their ships.'[14] In 1690 France could muster the greatest naval force she ever had. She was able in the same year at Beachy Head to beat the united fleets of the confederates, England and Holland. However, the triumph of the French navy was fairly short-lived. There were several reasons for its early decline. The financial difficulties of maintaining such an enormous military force at sea were no less considerable for a country which also had great military commitments on land than the difficulties of finding sufficient professional seaman for manning such a big fighting fleet. No less important a factor in the decline of the French navy and its more or less constant inferiority to the naval force of England and Britain were those immovable social cleavages embodied by Louis XIV in the constitution of his naval army in order to assure for himself the supreme control. Colbert's *Code des armées navales*, executed according to the wishes and orders of his master, was one of the best instances of a plan, very lucid and eminently intelligible as a blueprint, which defeated its own ends partly at least because the rivalries, the institutional conflicts – in short, the human relationships created by it – put a brake to its efficient working in practice. The main cleavage, the perpetual feud between civil and military officers, recruited from different social classes, weakened the French naval service in many ways. The higher civil officers had a seat in the councils of war. Their subordinates on board the ships down to the purser reported directly to them over the head of the military officers, and they were instructed to report everything of importance that happened during a cruise or during an action. In that way, constantly policed or (to use a more appropriate word) spied upon by those whom they regarded socially as their inferiors, the military officers of the French naval army were very reluctant to take any risks; they were noted in England for their personal courage, but also for their professional caution. Subject to a constant supervision characteristic of an absolutist regime, both officers and man were, as Pepys and many other Englishmen after him observed, naturally obedient and well disciplined; but it was a high price that had to be paid for these advantages: bureaucratic routine stifled to an extent the individual initiative of the military noblemen and gentlemen. Moreover, in the feud with their bourgeois rivals, they were more often than not on the defensive. With a very few exceptions the minister of the naval department was, up to the French Revolution, usually not a soldier but a civil administrator, taken from the upper bourgeoisie. The bourgeois section of the naval army, the hierarchy of civil officers, therefore on the whole had slightly the upper hand, though the court-influence of the aristocratic section could to certain extent make up for it. This ingenious system of ruling by divisions, which can be traced back to the Middle Ages, but which was fully developed and cast into its final mould by Louis XIV, made the military noblemen and gentlemen all the more 'class conscious'. They strenuously resisted even the slightest infringement of their privileges; they watched jealously over the conservation of everything that traditionally served as a distinguishing mark of their superior social rank. That they were harder pressed by other social groups than the English nobility and gentry was one reason more why they insisted on keeping aloof from the professional seamen and on drawing a strict demarcation line between appointments reserved for people *tirés du grand état* and the others (to the command of auxiliary craft and smaller vessels) open to people *du petit état*. It was one more reason why the French officer generally remained more of a soldier after the pattern of the land army and less of a seaman than the English naval officer.

However different in structure and character as the naval services of France and also of Spain were from England's, we should not lose sight of the underlying similarities. Socially, in all three countries the aristocracy ranked highest, and apart perhaps from the period of the Commonwealth its social superiority was never seriously disputed. In all the three countries, the social demarcations were far more overt than they are in the same countries today, inside their naval forces as outside. It is true that, in England, during the seventeenth and eighteenth century the dividing line separating those who were regarded as gentlemen from those who were not moved slowly forward from the gentry proper into the professional and commercial middle classes; wherever it stood at a given time, it was strenuously defended. During part of the eighteenth century it was only slightly less difficult for a man to rise from the forecastle to the quarterdeck, generally reserved for gentlemen and noblemen in the English navy, than it was in the naval service of France. However, there existed in England at that time nothing like Colbert's great *ordonnance* laying it down in so many words that the station leading up to the rank of a naval officer was open only to people of this or that social extraction. The official English regulations concerned with the conditions for promotion into the commissioned ranks, though sometimes distinguishing between gentlemen and others, were at that time never prohibitive with regard to the others. Seamen who had started at the bottom of the ladder were, during the eighteenth century, on the whole progressively less admitted into the commissioned ranks than before. But it was due not so much to the letter of the law as to a sort of common consent among the gentleman classes in control of promotion. In the same way, there existed during part of the eighteenth century inside the English officer corps a demarcation line very similar to that which in France segregated the officers of the *petit état* from those belonging to the *grand état*. An ordinary seaman who had worked his way up to the station of a warrant officer in the navy, or who had been brought up in the merchant service, could get a commission as 'master and commander' of a sloop or a bomb vessel; he would be called 'captain'. But in 99 cases out of a hundred he would never rise to the next station in the hierarchy of naval offices, that of a post-captain, which was, more pronouncedly even than that of lieutenant, reserved for gentlemen. Again there were no official regulations fixing this barrier inside the commissioned ranks; there was not even a name for it similar to the French distinction between officers of the small and the great estate. In all but fact it was an invisible barrier maintained by the more or less silent agreement among those who proposed and selected people for the higher appointments and hardly noticed by those who lived later. Yet, because it was never fixed by official regulations and never enunciated as a hard and fast rule, it was in a way more elastic and more adaptable to circumstances.

In fact, although strict demarcation lines between various estates and classes existed in England as in France, they were of different nature; they reflected the different political systems of the two countries. France was ruled by a power above all others, by a king intent on controlling everything by detailed regulations and by mutual jealousies of strictly divided rival classes. It was one of the ruling principles of this system to maintain these dividing lines, to emphasise them and to make them part of the law of the land. England on the other hand was ruled by a combination of groups and coteries, none of which – not even the King – stood clearly above all others. Much less, therefore, could be settled by a ruling from above, by state regulations, enforced by professional state officials; much more was left to be settled directly among the various groups interested in a matter either in parliament or outside. They were not kept apart in a more or less stationary form by a dominant power; they could constantly test their mutual strength, now battling with each other, now compromising on a point and forming coalitions against a third party; and the demarcation line between various groups and coteries and classes might shift according to their changing strength and fortune.

It is from this background that one has to view the different structure and development of the naval profession in France and England. It was not only the social tradition of the military caste in France, of the *noblesse d'épée*, and the superiority of the military profession, natural in a great continental country, which made French military men less willing and less capable than the English to combine with their duties some of those of a lower class; their social reserve, their endeavour to stick as far as possible to the traditional mark of their class as military men was intensified and, in a way, hardened by a political system based on the strict maintenance of the social status quo. With an absolute king in the key position, the fundament of the social scene became more or less petrified.[15] Changes were never allowed to affect its basic structure, upon which the power of the king rested; it needed a revolution to alter it. If necessary, they were projected by the government, executed according to plan; the king or his delegates gave the lead; the actors had to follow. Even social rivalries and feuds, like that between the *corps de l'épée* and the bourgeois *corps de la plume* in the navy, or in the wider social field between the *noblesse d'épée* and the bourgeois *noblesse de robe* did not lead to any institutional changes; they were kept smouldering; they remained stationary.

CONCLUSION: ENGLAND'S ADVANTAGE

England's political system on the other hand worked in a different and frequently opposite way. With a whole combination of social groups in power, the initiative of the government was necessarily more limited. The whole mode in which institutions developed and changes were brought about was different. The groups of people directly concerned in such a transformation gave the lead. Forms of relationship, social functions and offices that had sprung up among them more or less spontaneously, were after a certain time taken up by parliament or government and, perhaps in a modified form, fixed by statute and regulations. For that reason, the role played by the feud between gentlemen and seaman in the English navy was quite different from that played by the feud between civil and military officers in the French. It was by no means stationary. It had a direct influence upon the development of the naval profession, or to be more precise it was an essential part of it. The experience gained in this contest contributed greatly to the ultimate fusion between seamen's duties and military duties in most of the naval offices. Many forms of relationships established by government regulations had grown first spontaneously on board the ships. In fact this feud between military men and professional seamen, as well as the gradual coalescence of some of their characteristics, and the emergence of a special naval profession distinct from both was possible only under a political system less given to rule by strict regulations and divisions than in France.

Fragments

5

The Growing Costs of the Naval Establishment: Elizabeth and Cromwell Compared

The history of a profession is part of the social and economic history of its country. If the first stage gave rise to a specialised naval profession, the constant interdependency of the two maritime services (military and commercial) remained one of the basic factors in the development of this profession during the later stages. One need hardly dwell upon the fact that the growth of England's mercantile fleet as well as that of her foreign trade, once the division of labour between the two services was well established, became dependent on the parallel growth of England's military service at sea, the Navy. We are constantly reminded of that fact. Yet it is no less true, though perhaps less obvious, that the development of the Navy was equally dependent on a corresponding development of the mercantile service. It is hardly imaginable that a navy of the seize and strength demanded by the uninterrupted power rivalry could have been financially sustained without a proportionate growth of both England's foreign trade and its carrier, the merchant fleet. If we look only at the first stages of England's naval power it was already a big step from the amount which Queen Elizabeth spent on her navy in the early years of her reign, ranging from about £6,000 to £17,000 a year or even from the abnormally high naval expenditure of more than £92,000 in the year of the Armada,[1] to the equally abnormal amount of £1,400,000 that Cromwell spent on his Navy in 1652–3 (see table 1) or the £400,000 which James II regarded as a sort of minimum; and there were greater things to follow. The growing burden of England's military establishment at sea would in fact have been unbearable for the country without a corresponding growth of her commercial activities overseas, in connection, of course, with the growth of her own productive capacity. We encounter here another of these elementary screw mechanisms which play such an important part in every kind of historical development. The expanding commercial activities overseas and the growing merchant fleet needed for their support a military fleet proportionate in size, and *vice versa*. It is vain to ask whether the first move came from the one side or from the other; there were no separate moves at first. From small beginnings and a state when the same fleet more or less served both ends, military and commercial, the two branches, symbols of a progressing division of labour, developed into twin services, interdependent in their progress. Each move forward from the one side had to be followed, sooner or later, by a corresponding move from the other; and if one branch moved too far ahead of the other, in the long run, it was bound to fail. We have the example of the German Hansa towns, during part of the Middle Ages the most powerful commercial league in the Baltic and the North Sea, declining steadily when their neighbours grew stronger – for want, mainly, of a political and military power strong enough to back its treaties, its shipping and its overseas establishments. The development of a military fleet for the protection of commercial shipping and overseas trade was bound up in every country with the state of its central authorities. Germany, owing to her political weakness, was in fact the only country on the other side of the Channel unable for a long time to enter the race for overseas possessions and overseas trade.[2] Her political disunion and, in consequence, her inability to compete with her expanding neighbours put a brake to her economic development. On the other hand we have the example of Spain building up a powerful military fleet without developing to the same extent her commercial resources and her trading fleet. This disproportionate growth, too, proved fatal. In the long run she could not support the one without the other. One could almost say that, in their general outline though not in every detail, these basic conditions of the fleet first unfolding in two branches – those perpetual bonds between them – might serve as a small-scale model for the study of a wider problem: the interrelation between economic and political or military activities generally.

Table 1 Total government expenditure and naval expenditure under the Commonwealth

	Total expenditure (in round figures) £	Naval expenditure £
1652–3	2,600,000	1,400,000
1657–8	951,000	624,000
1658–9	1,517,000	848,000

Source: W. L. Clowes, *The Royal Navy: A History from the Earliest Times to the Present* (London: Sampson Low, Marston & Co., 1898), vol. II, p. 106.

Yet the interdependence between the two branches of the fleet was not restricted to these military and economic links. There were still other, even more direct ties linking the progress of the English navy to that of the merchant service. In times of war, and quite frequently also in peacetime, the military branch of the fleet had to rely on the other for part of her personnel. In fact the merchant service, in spite of its steady growth, was never quite able to provide the navy with all the men required in times of emergency in addition to those already employed by her.

The manning of the old sailing navy was a perpetual source of difficulties and troubles for all people concerned. Throughout the centuries it has provoked an endless flood of pamphlets and innumerable discussions in parliament; and it was by no means only the stubbornness or the inefficiency of those in power which perpetuated these difficulties and the irksome system of manning the Navy by impressment. There were some conditions inherent in the nature of a sailing fleet which made it an almost insoluble problem. Into the army people could be drafted from almost any profession in the land; whatever they might have done before, they could learn the art of a soldier in a fairly short time. Even the duties of an army officer could be performed quite well without long and specialised training at a period when fencing and pistol shooting were part of the qualifications of a gentleman. The situation was quite different with regard to the old navy.

> A soldier [said Captain Griffiths] springs up in six weeks or two months, fresh from the plough-tail; a seaman is not the mushroom of a day; he springs from long and regular apprenticeship and is then [the] only subject of his Majesty whose services the necessities of the state are compelled on every occasion of war, to enforce.[3]

At a time when a long-term policy with regard to the personnel was not or perhaps could not be attempted, one of the basic difficulties of manning the navy properly came from the fact that she needed professional seamen – skilled labourers – unlike the army. Under the pressure of parliament – that is to say, for political as well as financial reasons – the number of people employed in the navy in times of peace was usually kept as low as possible. Under the threat or at the actual outbreak of a war it had to be increased at all costs. The fluctuations in the number of seamen employed by the navy, therefore, were considerable. Before the war with France began in 1793 the Navy estimate provided wages and salaries for 20,000 seamen; 16,000 were added in the same year. In 1795 the figure had risen to 85,000, in 1796 to 100,000; it remained at about the same level till 1802. During the temporary lull that followed it fell in 1803 to 38,000, climbed up to 45,600 and then to 77,600 in the same year, remained at 78,000 in 1804, rose to 90,000 in 1805, to 98,600 in 1807, to 113,600 in 1810; there it remained till 1812, falling again to 74,000 in 1814 and, finally, to 24,000 in 1816.[4] As, on the whole, only professional seamen could do this work properly, the field of recruitment was restricted to the fishing trade and the merchant service. Part of the people employed there had to be protected from the press. The effects of this competition for men between the military and the trading fleet were often quite noticeable in peacetime. Yet, even in times of war, it was impossible to denude fishing and trading vessels of all hands. Moreover, the merchant service itself had difficulties in attracting sufficient people. At least from the beginning of the eighteenth century onwards, the rate of increase of England's foreign trade and commercial shipping was greater than that of her seafaring population. Part of a merchantman's crew was, from the time of William of Orange, frequently made up of foreigners; during the later part of the century, it seems, it was usually a quarter, if not more. In that way the capacity of the merchant service to rear a reserve of seaman for the navy was further limited, although in times of emergency the officer of the press was apt to overlook the foreign nationality of an able bodied seaman, just as he was not wholly averse from pressing landsmen. Various measures were taken to overcome these limitations. Sometimes it was enacted that foreigners employed in British merchant ships could already be naturalised after two years' service.[5] Over certain periods British merchant ships were allowed to have three-quarters of their crews made up of foreigners,[6] thus setting English-born seamen free for service in the navy. Another way to make up for this shortage of professional seamen was the establishment of marine regiments, regular troops, not capable of taking over the part of skilled seamen, but trained to do part of the fighting on board ships. Some, though by no means all, of the harsh practices to which seamen during the eighteenth and part of the nineteenth century were usually exposed in the navy may be also explained by this perpetual shortage of man. For fear of desertion, they were quite frequently not allowed ashore when the ship returned from a journey to a home port; they were shifted from one ship to the other, as long as they were needed, often for years without leave, without being able to see their families, unless their wives came to pay them a visit on board the ship. Moreover, according to government regulations they were not permitted to receive more than part of their wages – if they were paid at all – before being finally dismissed. All these practices were, of course, made possible only by their complete lack of political influence. As it was, they were kept in the navy for lack of sufficient reserves almost like prisoners, at least in times of war.

6

On Institutions

We usually do not give much thought to the question of why an institution became what it is at present. In general we content ourselves with describing its various stages and, underlying these descriptions, there seems to be a general idea – unchecked, yet firmly rooted in our mind – that each of these stages is the work of one or several great and powerful personalities with whose names it is linked in our history books. That may be so. However, if we enquire into the reasons why a change was found necessary at each particular stage, we would see that they were always provoked by flaws and maladjustment in the working of these institutions – certain dissensions and conflicts between various groups or factions setting the problem for which a solution had to be sought. We can hardly hope to understand these solutions unless we inquire into the nature of the dissensions, maladjustment and social conflicts behind them; for, by posing the problem, they served at the same time as the driving force for the development of that institution. In fact none of the institutions among which we live developed in any other way. Flaws and conflicts are just as important a characteristic of their structure as are adjustments. They are all the outcome of past struggles, rivalries and dissensions; they are all embodying either the defeat of one of the contending groups and factions or a compromise between them. They are nothing more and nothing less than fixed forms of relationships between various groups of people and, in a narrower sense, regarded in a smaller circle between various individuals cast together by their commission to the duties and responsibilities embodied in them, forms of relationship enforced by law and the power behind it. We can always see them grow from a stage where the initial conflict between groups and factions around them or their representatives, the individuals within, is quite open; and when the relationship between these individuals, the division of duties between them, is vague in outline and undifferentiated compared with later stages. We can observe how they develop through failures and experimental forms and perhaps periods of temporary decay into a more clearly stable defined mould of relationships with a greater and better regulated division of duties and responsibilities.

One may doubt whether 'institution' is the proper word for the naval establishment and the occupation of a naval officer. But whatever word we choose, the driving forces of their development are the same as those of other institutions. We may say that the Tudor kings, or more especially Henry VIII, 'created' the English navy; but we must also see that the problem was set for him by the growing Atlantic rivalry into which England was becoming unavoidably entangled. We may fix the precise period at which the office of a naval lieutenant or of a midshipman was established; but at the same time one cannot help seeing that the fuel for that constant drive towards a greater differentiation of duties on board a man-of-war, in the course of which these offices emerged, was also furnished by the latent or open conflicts between the Atlantic powers and, moreover, that their character as a gentleman's job or a seaman's job was one of the issues at stake in the battle between seaman and gentlemen. The same is true for the formation and especially for the social character of all the other naval ranks. With regard to naval ranks, it may perhaps be possible to establish by statistical means how many of their holders came from the forecastle and how many were gentlemen starting their naval career on the quarterdeck – though, of course, over long stretches of naval history for most of the naval ranks the material for such a statistical survey is rather scanty and fragmentary;

yet even if it was more complete, such a survey could at the best confirm what has to be explained by other means. For the ascent to the rank of a naval officer was not simply left to the individual members of the different sections of society. The social character of these ranks and, therefore, the recruiting and selection of their personnel, were at each period part of an established order. It was determined by the institutional channels for entrance and promotion provided for persons of different social origin and upbringing. These channels, however, and with them the selection machinery, came into shape gradually amidst many conflicts and dissension, and the initial struggle between seamen and gentlemen had a great share in the growth. In fact it is only by inquiring into the institutional development of the navy and in its causes that we are able to understand how and why its various functions and responsibilities were divided in this or that way among members of different sections of society.

7

The Last Act: Elias's Scenario for a Play about Drake and Doughty

The problem of the last act is whether the love feast and Holy Communion can sustain the tension without which a last act must fall flat. Do not be deceived. The actual plot, the vision of the last act, in itself, is more than enough to sustain the tension. The difficulty is the execution. The vision is clear.

The central vision is that of the two men seated perhaps with four, perhaps with others on simple wooden benches before a table not unlike the men in Leonardo's *Last Supper*. Drake, Doughty and the Priest. For the two men what is to come is clear. If there is still a small voice of hope against hope that a way other than Doughty's death may be found, it is Drake's rather than Doughty's. Doughty goes with his eyes open to his death and almost chooses it. At no time before did his deep affection and friendship for Drake express itself so clearly and unsentimentally:

> I could not have acted otherwise. I would act again in the same way. I cannot betray myself. I have not been wrong. Nor has Drake. How wonderful a leader of men he is. A tale from Ireland. He will achieve what he has set out to do. He will find the lucky island, the little paradise for man and for England. But he could not do it with me on board. I cannot bend my knees.
>
> There are only two possibilities. To send me back. We cannot spare the ships. And I could not help to make my case against him as I have made it here. Drake may offer to send him back. But Doughty declines:

I would only go before the Queen's court. There would be the court intrigues. The partisans of Walsingham and Burghley will tear me and the others here and there. So he can't send me back. The second possibility is to take me further on the journey. I do not want to go. He may protect me against his tarpaulins. He cannot protect me against myself. I cannot submit to his orders. I am his equal. I do not acknowledge anyone above me here. So there remains only one solution to which you all agreed.

I am the lamb; I go my way if you all are to find what you are looking for. I have to go – for your sake. Someone has to go and Drake assures him: We will achieve what we have set before us. We will bring the good tiding back to England.

They take the cake together. They drink from the same vessel. They embrace. Doughty is led away. Margaret and one of the younger gentlemen are crying quietly. Drake folds his hands for a short time, praying, then with a short resolve he asks for the boatswain and master to be brought before him with clear resolve. While they are being fetched – while one hears their name being called out behind the scene to come to the Admiral, Doughty's young brother burst in the room with drawn sword. Shouting 'murderer, assassin'. That he has betrayed his trust is his accusation against Drake. He never believed it. He is crying and shouting. As his men attempt to lay hands on the boy Drake winks to let him go and stand unarmed before him. He wants to be sent back. Drake quite unsentimentally: No! You will come with us. I cannot have accusers try my name while I am absent. Hoist the sail. There will be sunshine . . .

But this central scene is interlaced with smaller scenes which express the doubts and fears of others who do not yet know, in that respect like the audience, what is to come. The gentlemen make plans to rescue Doughty. John Winter is being approached and, although far from favourable to Drake, equally far from risking his neck. Etcetera.

Drake is not very tall and he begins to get a little too full around the middle. Doughty is taller, handsomer, more cultured and educated, of course, and also more obviously intelligent. Drake is much slower than Doughty in understanding, and especially in understanding implications and allusions. Think of the scene where he at first does not understand what the other says; and, in fact, never understands and, as he feels confused and unable to cope, he bursts out violently and beats Doughty. In fact Doughty, beaten, obviously nearing defeat, never ceases to taunt him and to show his intellectual superiority. It is as if he wants to make Drake lose his balance. Thus in gaining his own kind of victory, he also achieves his own destruction; and he knows it.

Drake's weapons and Drake's superiority are of an entirely different kind. With all the doubts and uncertainties on the surface which come his way, deeper down he never doubts; he knows what he wants, he knows where he is going and he knows that he is going to achieve it. He is the leader of the expedition as of right. Of course the Queen wanted him and him alone to be in command; of that he is quite certain. For the Queen's Majesty being nearer to God than any other mortal, knows of course, what only God and he himself (Drake) knows: that he cannot fail. He is going to defeat the Spaniard, to take their gold whenever it can be done without impairing the greater purpose of his journey; he is going to find new and rich lands for England, as rich as or richer in gold and treasures and beauty and women than the Spanish possessions. And he is going to be the second man in this world to circumnavigate the earth. And knowing his purpose and his mission without a doubt, he is of course quite certain; in case of doubt everybody else has to obey. One of Doughty's companions at one time says it quite clearly: if one could only shake the unshakeable confidence which he has in himself; and, of course, which as a result his men have in him. And they try – not Doughty himself, but some of the gentlemen – they set about cautiously, but systematically to undermine his confidence, or at least to try;

Doughty has actually told them, with an anecdote from his Irish time with Drake, that they will never succeed; but they do not believe him; and after all they have little choice; for now they are alone among the hostile mariners, how are they ever to get back to England if he goes on and on and on further West and West and West, further away from the homeland, for weeks and months and maybe for years, what are they to do in order to shake his resolution to go around the world, in spite of all the treasures which they have already collected and which would make the adventurers at home and on board ship quite happy if they only had their share tucked away safely in England. And so they try to shake the belief of his people in him whenever they can, with little success. And so there is nothing to do but to challenge his right to take decisions alone; and they put it to Doughty that he must be the bearer of this challenge. And Doughty is reluctant. And Drake suspects; and as the tension grows, there is also growing in Drake's mind the idea that if he is to succeed, he, like Magellan before him, has to bring a sacrifice to the dark powers of destruction so that they cannot do him any harm.

Appendix to Chapter 5

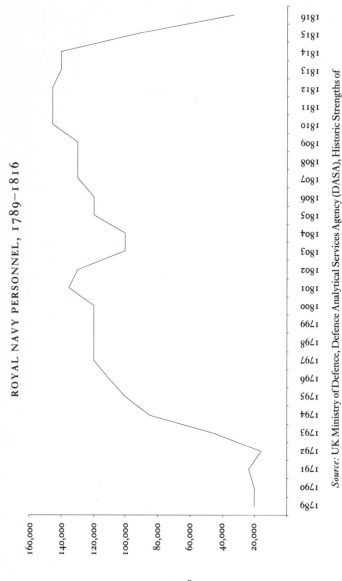

ROYAL NAVY PERSONNEL, 1789–1816

Source: UK Ministry of Defence, Defence Analytical Services Agency (DASA), Historic Strengths of UK Regular Forces database, 1 October 1998. This figure has been supplied by the editors.

Textual Variants

Sentences in chapter 1 to which minor amendments have been made by the editors for the sake of clarity are indicated in the text by a superscript letter. The original readings that appeared in the *British Journal of Sociology* in 1950 are given below.

Page

29[a]   In retrospect . . . evaporates.] In retrospect, the latter comes to life only when seen together with the former. If one comes face to face, behind the more impersonal facade, with people struggling, often in vain, to adjust their inherited institutional framework with all its incongruities to what they feel to be their own needs, then the atmosphere so often surrounding old institutions in history books, the atmosphere of museum pieces, loses itself.

34[b]   'for specialised . . . warfare'] specialised for warfare.

45[c]   'Admiral . . . Bedford'] Edward Russell, the father of Admiral Russell, later Earl of Orford (1653–1727), was a younger brother of the first Duke of Bedford.

Notes

Introduction: Elias's Studies of the Naval Profession

1 The Introduction is adapted from Moelker's article 'Norbert Elias, maritime supremacy and the naval profession: on Elias's unpublished studies in the genesis of the naval profession', *British Journal of Sociology* 54: 3 (2003), pp. 373–90.

2 This topic is actually dealt with adequately in M. Lewis, *England's Sea-officers: The Story of the Naval Profession* (London: George Allen & Unwin, 1939), to which Elias does not refer.

3 NE Archive 503; see the bibliography (pp. 156–7) for a list of the relevant folders in the Elias papers in Marbach.

4 See also R. Moelker, 'The last knights', in H. Kirkels, W. Klinkert and R. Moelker (eds), *ARMS 2003 Officer Education: The Road to Athens* (Breda: Royal Netherlands Military Academy, 2003), pp. 81–99.

5 NE Archive 505.

6 Norbert Elias and Eric Dunning, *Quest for Excitement: Sport and Leisure in the Civilising Process* (Oxford: Blackwell, 1986 [Collected Works, vol. 7]); Elias, *The Germans: Power Struggles and the Development of Habitus in the Nineteenth and Twentieth Centuries* (Cambridge: Polity, 1996 [Studies on the Germans, Collected Works, vol. 11]).

7 A. M. Carr-Saunders and P. A. Wilson, *The Professions* (Oxford: Clarendon Press, 1933).

8 Talcott Parsons, 'Professions and social structure' (1939), in his *Essays in Sociological Theory* (rev. edn, Glencoe, IL: Free Press, 1954), pp. 34–49; see also 'A sociologist looks at the legal profession', ibid., pp. 372–85, and 'Social Structure and dynamic process: the case of modern medical practice', ch. 10 of Parsons, *The Social System* (Glencoe, IL: Free Press, 1951), pp. 428–79.

9 Elias, 'Professions', in Julius Gould and William L. Kolb (eds), *A Dictionary of the Social Sciences* (New York, Free Press, 1964), p. 542.

10 But see Parsons, 'Professions and social structure', for a subtle discussion rejecting the dichotomous opposition of 'altruism' and the pursuit of

'self-interest' – a rejection of static polarities that was generally a characteristic of Elias's own thinking.

11 Carr-Saunders and Wilson, *The Professions*, included among others patent agents, dentists, nurses, midwives, veterinary surgeons, pharmacists, opticians, masseurs, mine managers, engineers, scientists, surveyors, accountants, actuaries, teachers, journalists and – of special interest in this context, the merchant navy. They did not cover the military and naval professions, since their interest was mainly in the workings of professional associations.

12 Terence J. Johnson, *Professions and Power* (London: Macmillan, 1972); Geoffrey Hurd (ed.), *Human Societies: An Introduction to Sociology* (London: Routledge & Kegan Paul, 1973).

13 David Marquand, *Decline of the Public* (Cambridge: Polity, 2004).

14 Elias's few published essays prior to 1939 are collected in *Early Writings* (Dublin: UCD Press, 2006 [Collected Works, vol. 1]); even including his 1922 Breslau doctoral thesis, they constitute quite a slim volume.

15 See Stephen Mennell, 'Elias and the counter-ego', *History of the Human Sciences* 19: 2 (2006), pp. 73–91.

16 Elias, *The Court Society* (Dublin: UCD Press, 2006 [Collected Works, vol. 2]).

17 N. Elias and J. L. Scotson, *The Established and the Outsiders: A Sociological Enquiry into Community Problems* (London: Frank Cass, 1965 [Collected Works, vol. 4]).

18 Elias, *Reflections on a Life* (Cambridge: Polity, 1994 [*Autobiographical Essays and Interviews*, Collected Works, vol. 17]), p. 64.

19 Cas Wouters, 'Ja, ja, ik was nog niet zoo'n beroerde kerel, die zoo'n vrind had', in Han Israëls, Mieke Komen and Abram de Swaan (eds), *Over Elias: Herinneringen en anekdotes* (Amsterdam: Het Spinhuis, 1993), p. 10.

20 Johan Goudsblom, *De sociologie van Norbert Elias* (Amsterdam: Meulenhoff, 1987), p. 221, n. 18.

21 C. J. Lammers, 'Strikes and mutinies: a comparative study of organisational conflicts between rulers and ruled', *Administrative Science Quarterly* 14: 4 (1969) pp. 558–72; G. Teitler, *Toepassing van geweld* (Meppel: Boom, 1972); G. Teitler, *De wording van het professionele officierscorps* (Rotterdam: Universitaire Pers Rotterdam, 1974); G. Teitler, *The Genesis of the Professional Officers' Corps* (London: Sage, 1977).

22 Morris Janowitz, *The Professsional Soldier: A Social and Political Portrait.* (Glencoe, IL: Free Press, 1960), p. 23.

23 G. Caforio (ed.), 'The military profession in Europe', *Current Sociology* 42: 3 (1994), pp. 107–29; G. Caforio (ed.), *The Sociology of the Military* (Cheltenham: Edward Elgar, 1998); J. Kuhlmann, *The Present and Future of the Military Profession: Views of European Officers* (Strausberg: Sowi, 1996).

24 J. A. A. van Doorn, *Sociologie van de organisatie* (Leiden: Stenfert Kroese, 1956); J. A. A. van Doorn, 'The officer corps: a fusion of profession and organisation', *Archives Européennes de Sociologie* 6: 2 (1965), pp. 262–82; J. A. A. van Doorn and M. Janowitz, *Armed Forces and Society: Sociological Essays* (The Hague: Mouton, 1968).

25 J. Goudsblom, 'Een kritiek op *Moderne sociologie* [by J. A. A. van Doorn and C. J. Lammers]', *Sociologische Gids* 9: 1 (1962), pp. 28–39; J. A. A. van Doorn and C. J. Lammers, 'Repliek', *Sociologische Gids* 9: 1 (1962), pp. 39–48; J. Goudsblom, '*Moderne sociologie*: de systematiek geanalyseerd', *Amsterdams Sociologisch Tijdschrift* 6: 3 (1979), pp. 371–98; J. A. A. van Doorn and C. J. Lammers, '*Moderne sociologie*: de bezwaren van Goudsblom', *Amsterdams Sociologisch Tijdschrift* 7: 3 (1980), pp. 339–43; J. Goudsblom, 'Nawoord', *Amsterdams Sociologisch Tijdschrift* 7: 3 (1980), pp. 344–5.

26 As a scientific explanation the analysis by Elias complies more with the principle of parsimony than Teitler's. See R. Moelker, 'Beroep marine-officier: studies van Norbert Elias en Ger Teitler over het ontstaan van het beroep van marineofficier', *Marineblad* 113: 4 (2003), pp. 114–23.

27 Elias, 'Drake en Doughty: de ontwikkeling van een conflict', trans. Nelleke Fuchs-van Maaren, *De Gids* 140: 5–6 (1977), pp. 223–37.

28 Hurd, *Human Societies*; C. Dandeker, 'From patronage to bureaucratic control: the case of the naval officer in English society, 1780–1850', *British Journal of Sociology* 29: 3 (1978), pp. 300–20.

29 J. Goudsblom and S. J. Mennell (eds), *The Norbert Elias Reader: A Biographical Selection* (Oxford: Blackwell, 1998), pp. 81–3.

30 Elias, 'Etudes sur les origines de la profession de marin', *Les Champs de Mars* 13: 4 (2003), pp. 7–23; 'Estudos sobre a gênese da profissão naval: cavalheiros e tarpaulins', *Mana* 7: 1 (2001), pp. 89–116.

31 The typescript of this speech comprises 21 pages, which Elias had re-worked and translated into German; NE Archive: MISC-D X = Paris 3: 2.

32 Johan Goudsblom, 'Responses to Norbert Elias's work in England, Germany, the Netherlands and France', in P. R. Gleichmann, J. Goudsblom and H. Korte (eds), *Essays for/Aufsätze für Norbert Elias* (Amsterdam: Stichting Amsterdams Sociologisch Tijdschrift, 1977), p. 48.

33 J. D. Davies, *Gentlemen and Tarpaulins: The Officers and Men of the Restoration Navy* (Oxford: Clarendon Press, 1991).

34 Norbert Elias, 'Introduction: sociology and historiography', *Court Society*, pp. 3–38.

35 Émile Durkheim, *The Rules of Sociological Method* (Glencoe, IL: Free Press, 1964 [1895]), p. 139.

36 Teitler, *Genesis*, describes the position of the Dutch navy in a most elaborate manner. Elias, in fact, merely notes that the position of the Dutch is different from the French. He states that in many ways the Dutch are comparable to the English.

37 Teitler, *Genesis*, pp. 112–24.

38 P. Padfield, *Maritime Supremacy and the Opening of the Western Mind* (London: Pimlico, 2000).

39 NE Archive 510: 34.

40 NE Archive 510: 8–9.

41 Elias, *The Civilising Process* (Oxford: Blackwell, 2000 [*On the Process of Civilisation*, Collected Works, vol. 3]), pp. 312–44; Teitler, *Genesis*, p. 31.

42 Elias, *Civilising Process*, p. 320.

43 The 'royal mechanism' has some affinity with Georg Simmel's famous discussion (in K. H. Wolff (ed.), *The Sociology of Georg Simmel* (Glencoe: Free Press, 1950), p. 145–69) of triadic relationships, and especially of the principle of *tertius gaudens*.

44 Elias, Introduction to Elias and Dunning, *Quest for Excitement*, pp. 26–40.

45 Elias, *Court Society*, chapter 9.

46 Elias and Scotson, *The Established and the Outsiders*.

47 Elias, *Civilising Process*, p. 68.

48 Appendix, NE Archive 518.

49 NE Archive 517.

50 These objectives of the study show a remarkable parallel with the studies which Elias published together with Dunning on sports (fox hunting, boxing, soccer) and leisure time (Elias and Dunning, *Quest for Excitement*). In the studies of sports, the object is also the psycho- and sociogenesis of English culture.

51 That is why Elias's earliest work uses the terms *Verflechtungsfigur* or *Menschenflechtwerk* (interweaving of humans). In modern translations of *The Civilising Process*, *Menschenflechtwerk* is translated as 'figuration'. Elias briefly described a 'figuration' as 'the changing pattern created by the

players as a whole – not only by their intellects but by their whole selves, the totality of their dealings in their relationships with each other. It can be seen that this figuration forms a flexible lattice-work of tensions. The interdependence of the players, which is a prerequisite of their forming a figuration, may be an interdependence of allies or of opponents.' (Elias, *What is Sociology?* (London: Hutchinson, 1978, p. 130 [Collected Works, vol. 5]).

52 G. C. Homans, 'The small warship', *American Sociological Review* 11: 3 (1946), pp. 294–300.

53 NE Archive 513.

54 Elias occasionally used the word 'dialectic' to describe his method, but on the whole avoided the term because of its Hegelian and transcendental associations.

55 NE Archive: MISC-D X = Paris 3: 13.

56 N. A. M. Rodger, *The Safeguard of the Sea*, vol. 1, 660–1649, of *A Naval History of Britain* (London: HarperCollins and National Maritime Museum, 1997); N. A. M. Rodger, *The Command of the Ocean*, vol. 2, 1649–1815, of *A Naval History of Britain* (London: Allen Lane and National Maritime Museum, 2004).

57 Padfield, *Maritime Supremacy*.

58 Charles Tilly, 'Reflections on the history of European state-making', in Tilly (ed.), *The Formation of National States in Western Europe* (Princeton, NJ: Princeton University Press, 1975), p. 42.

I

Gentlemen and Tarpaulins

This chapter consists of the article originally published in the *British Journal of Sociology* 1: 4 (1950), pp. 291–309. In a note at the foot of the first page, Elias stated:

This is the first of three studies in the origins and the early development of the career of naval officers in England. It shows the initial situation in which members of the nascent profession were recruited from two very different social groups. The second study deals with tensions and conflicts between these two groups; the third with their gradual integration and the emergence of a more unified hierarchy of naval offices combining to some extent the functions and methods of training of both groups. In addition, a brief comparison with the early development of the naval profession in France shows some of the interrelations between the development and characteristics of naval professions and those of the countries to which they belong.

These studies are based on research undertaken some years ago for the Social Research Division of the London School of Economics. I am greatly indebted to Mr H. L. Beales for his friendly advice and encouragement.

1 'Gear and apparel' in a literal as well as metaphorical sense, for professionals such as lawyers, clergy and military officers do wear uniforms or robes. – eds.

2 'I shall send you books so that your children can read them.'

The headman said, 'Thank you for your gift', and raised his hands in salute, as one must do whenever anyone offers you something in Limbo. But then he dropped his hands and said with a touch of impatience, 'Is not that like the man who gave the village a tiger and then gave the village a gun to shoot it with?'

A roar of approval . . . came from his listeners. 'We have no books and so we do not need to read.'

From Aubrey Menen, *The Prevalence of Witches* (London: Chatto & Windus, 1947), p. 94.

3 A. M. Carr-Saunders and P. A. Wilson, *The Professions* (Oxford: Clarendon Press, 1933), p. 297, where this interdependence has been noted, though with a stronger emphasis on one factor, the progress of research.

4 M. Ginsberg, 'The work of L. T. Hobhouse', in J. A. Hobson and M. Ginsberg (eds), *L. T. Hobhouse: His Life and Work* (London: Allen & Unwin, 1931), p. 158: 'The most common method of operation in large groups is strictly comparable to what in individual psychology is called trial and error. The accommodation of partial purposes to one another, their interrelation and correlation, is brought about by a series of efforts at adjustment within which the external observer may perchance detect a principle which the agents themselves certainly could not formulate. There is in short a point-by-point adjustment but no comprehensive or settled purpose.'

5 Thomas Babington Macaulay, *The History of England* (10th edn, London: Longman, Brown, Green & Longmans, 1854), vol. I, p. 304: 'There were gentlemen and there were seamen in the navy of Charles

the Second. But the seamen were not gentlemen; and the gentlemen were not seamen.' – eds

6 That is, until it surrendered. – eds.

7 Here Elias misattributes Macaulay's famous remark to Samuel Pepys (1633–1703), the celebrated author of the *Diary* (1660–9), and English naval administrator. Pepys was Clerk of the Acts to the Navy Board, 1660–73 and Secretary to the Admiralty, 1673–9, 1684–9. In 1683 he was sent to Tangier to assist in the evacuation of the English colony there, and travelled back through Spain. He also served as a Member of Parliament and as President of the Royal Society. – eds.

8 W. Monson, *The Naval Tracts of Sir William Monson in Six Books*, ed. M. Oppenheim, vol. IV (London: Navy Records Society [Pub. NRS, vols 22, 23, 43, 45, 47], 1913), p. 14.

9 Ibid., p. 15.

10 'Look at Drake. His reputation is so great that his countrymen flock to him to share his booty.' – *Cal. S. P. Ven.*, 20 Aug. 1588.

11 The term 'commander', throughout that period, referred to the actual function of people, not to any specific rank. It could be applied to all people in command of a ship.

12 'Tarpaulin', a piece of canvas washed over with tar, was at that time what one might call the overall of the ordinary seaman. It had many uses. It could be employed as cover during the night. It could provide shelter from sun and wind or serve as a raincoat. So, from the name of what they used as a garment, 'Tarpaulin' became the sobriquet of the men. Being rather a long and unhandy word for a nickname, in course of time it became 'tar' pure and simple.

13 Monson, *Naval Tracts*, IV, p. 24.

14 Monson stressed the difference between the authority of captains in the Royal Navy who 'had power from a General' and that of 'private captains' who had merely been granted letters of reprisal. The latter was in exactly the same position as the master and other mariners whether he was a professional seaman or a gentleman. For they all went out 'on their own adventure' and received no pay. 'Therefore they will', wrote Monson, who was obviously speaking from experience, 'tie the captain to the same conditions, in his diet, . . . as themselves are tied. His authority is little better than the captain in a pirate' (Monson, *Naval Tracts*, IV, p. 17). The difference between privateers and pirates was at that time not as great as it may appear to us. The former plundered, burned and destroyed foreign ships

with the permission of Queen or King, the latter without it. Capt. John Smith, in his *The Generall Historie of Virginia, New England & the Summer Isles* (Glasgow: MacLehose, 1907 [1624]), chap. 28, mentioned a number of Elizabethan sea-officers who in King James's time for lack of employment, because they 'were poore and had nothing but from hand to mouth', became pirates and were 'mercifully pardoned' when the King again needed experienced officers for his navy. [Elias himself mentioned a 1629 edition of Smith's book. – eds.]

15 Monson, *Naval Tracts*, IV, p. 14.

16 Samuel Pepys, *Naval Minutes*, ed. J. R. Tanner (London: Navy Records Society [Pub. NRS, vol. 60], 1926), p. 119.

17 S. D'Ewes, *The Journal of Sir Simonds D'Ewes: from the First Recess of the Long Parliament to the Withdrawal of King Charles from London*, ed. Willson Havelock Coates (New Haven: Yale University Press, 1942), p. 348, 10 Jan. 1641 (new style: 1642): 'A proposition came from the saylers and marriners to bee with us too morrow to defend the Parliament by water with muskets and other ammunitions in severall vessels which was accepted by us.'

A pamphlet, 'The Seaman's Protestation . . . concerning their Ebbing and Flowing to and from the Parliament House at Westminster, the 11th of January 1642', also indicates how strong was the feeling among the seamen of the navy that the cause of parliament, and of the City of London, was their own cause.

> a rumour being spread amongst us that that great Court was in fear to be dissolved, and knowing too well the happiness of this Kingdom consists in their services, remembering the words of Arch-bishop Cranmer, a Martyr of ever blessed memory, which were: Wo be to England when there is no Parliament, we seeing and heareing the whole City to be in compleat arms, presently turned freshwater soldiers, and with as sudden expedition as we could, attended by water their progress thither, and joyned our thunder of powder with the City Muskets, at their entrance into the House (the Temple of our safety), to the terrour we hope of all Papists and the Lands Enemies. . . . We who are alwayes abroad can best tell no government upon the Earth is comparable to it; . . . Witnesse the heavie and lamentable distractions in France, Spain and Germanie for want of them or the like Government. . . . Now the kingdom is involved in a civil war and a mighty Army of Papists (and

137

Atheists) contrary to the known Lawes of the Land are in Arms against the Parliament, if they could, to destroy the same and so trample the Common Laws and the COMMONS of England under foot, and to make us all slaves in our Religion, immunities and priviledges. It behoves us that are seamen to bestir us and looke about us the better and the rather because we, and who but we, are to manage the *Navy* of Ships which are and ever have beene accompted the brazen Walles of the Kingdom against Forrainne invasion . . .

Sir John Laughton, in a paper 'Historians and naval history' (in J. S. Corbett and H. J. Edwards (eds), *Naval and Military Essays* (Cambridge: Cambridge University Press, 1914), pp. 3–22) complaining, on good grounds, that the influence on England's national life attributed to the navy in historical studies was usually confined to battles won at sea and maintaining that, in fact, this influence was far greater and wider, gave among others the following example (p. 7):

it is, I think, familiarly known that in the Civil War of the seventeenth century, the Navy adhered to the Parliament, but as no battles were fought, the advantage to the Parliament was believed to be trifling, if not negligible. It was left for Dr Gardiner, after more than two hundred years, to show that it was really the determining factor of the struggle; but even Gardiner did not consider it necessary to examine why the Navy took the Parliamentary side.

[See B. Capp, *Cromwell's Navy* (Oxford: Clarendon Press, 1989 – eds.]
18 Richard Gibson, a clerk in the Navy office at the time of Pepys and an ardent partisan of the seamen, in a memorandum (quoted by John Charnock, in the Preface to his *History of Marine Architecture* (3 vols, London: R. Faulder, etc., 1800–2), I, pp. lxxxix, xcii.) compared the attitudes and qualifications of gentlemen officers and seamen officers. Though obviously biased, the comparison is, in some respects, quite instructive.

A gentleman is put into comand of (suppose a) 4th rate shipp, complement 200 men: he shall bring neare 20 landmen into the shipp, as his footmen, taylor, barber, fidlers, decayed kindred, voluntier gentleman, or acquaintance, as companions. These shall have the accommodation of a master's mate, midshipman, quartermaster, master trumpeter, coxswaine etc. and too often their pay. . . . Now all that gentlemen captaines bring aboard with them, are of bishop Williams's opinion, that Providence made man to live ashore, and it is necessity that drives him to sea. When on the contrary, a seaman, as soon as hee has comand of a 4th rate shipp of 200, has none belonging to him but such as devout themselves to the sea as to a trade. . . .

A seaman captain takes up less of the shipp for his accomodation.

A gentleman captain claims the sterridge for his grandeur, quarter deck for his jarrs, pidgeons etc.

A seaman is familiar amongst his men, talking to severall on the watch, is upon deck all night in foul weather, gives the most active a dram of his bottle. . . .

A gentleman has a sentinall at his great cabbin doore (to keepe silence in the belfry) and oft times beates his master for not comeing to him forthwith when hee rings his bell in the night. . . .

[A more complete and accurate transcription of Gibson's memorandum is found in 'Extracts from a Commissioner's Notebook', in Sir John Knox Laughton (ed.), *Naval Miscellany*, vol. II (London: Navy Records Society, 1912 [Pub. NRS vol. 40]) – eds]

19 Samuel Pepys, *The Tangier Papers* (London: Navy Records Society [Pub. NRS, vol. 73], 1935), p. 135.

20 J. Cremer, *Ramblin' Jack: The Journal of Captain John Cremer, 1700–1774* (London: Jonathan Cape, 1936), pp. 45 ff.

21 Ibid., pp. 33 ff. John Cremer's father made his living as master of merchantmen. His father's brother was a captain in the navy, his cousin a naval lieutenant. His mother was the daughter of a master rope-maker 'living high' and keeping his coach and livery. His mother's sister was married to 'Captain Maine, uncle to Admirall Maine'. He was brought up by an aunt who was first married to a Captain (without specification), then to a storekeeper in the Customs-house whose nephew was a naval captain. His grandmother, widow of the master-rope-maker, married for a second time an 'old gentleman who had two sons, lieutenants in the navy, and three daughters, one of whom was married to a captain of an East-India-man, one to a master of a merchantman and the third to a wealthy farmer'.

22 E. Barlow, *Barlow's Journal of his Life at Sea in King's Ships, East & West Indiamen & other Merchantmen from 1659 to 1703* (London: Hurst & Blackett, 1934), II, p. 328.

NOTES TO PP. 42-43

23 G. Penn, *Memorials of the Professional Life and Times of Sir William Penn, Admiral and General of the Fleet, During the Interregnum, Admiral, and Commissioner of the Admiralty and Navy, after the Restoration: from 1644 to 1670* (London: Duncan, 1833), I, p. 3.

24 *DNB.*

25 From the reign of Elizabeth, the Royal Navy was organised into three squadrons, the Red, White and Blue. Gradually this developed into a system of precedence with nine ranks of admiral, from Rear Admiral of the Blue through Rear Admiral of the White, Rear Admiral of the Red, Vice Admiral of the Blue and so on up to the Admiral of the Red squadron, who was known as Admiral of the Fleet. The division into three squadrons was abandoned in 1864, but a vestige of it is seen in the three British naval ensigns – White (Royal Navy), Blue (Naval Reserve), and Red (Merchant Navy). – eds

26 Penn, *Memorials*, p. 3.

27 Pepys, *Tangier Papers*, p. 228.

28 The top layer of the commercial classes was at that period represented by the governors and directors of the great trading companies, especially of the East India Company. In Queen Elizabeth's charter of 1600 neither the governor nor any of the 24 directors of this company was designated as 'gentleman'; in that of James I the governor was a knight, but the 24 directors were still plain citizens. In Charles II's charter of 1661 the governor and 11 of the 24 directors were called 'knights', one director was a peer, another was styled as 'esquire' and the rest as 'gentlemen' (India Office Library, Quarto of Charters, quoted in W. W. Hunter, *History of India* (London: Longmans, 1900), II, p. 188). This is one example of the transformation in the course of which the cleavage between the upper and upper middle classes became less, that between the latter and the lower classes more pronounced.

29 Barlow, *Journal.*

30 The famous story of how he swam as a boy with important dispatches in his mouth through the line of the enemy fire is in all probability apocryphal. Neither the tracts written in praise of Shovel shortly after his death, nor Campbell [John Campbell, *Lives of the British Admirals*, 4 vols (London: J. & H. Pemberton, T. Waller, 1742–4)], from the middle of the eighteenth century, mentioned it. John Charnock, in his *Biographia Navalis*, 6 vols (London: R. Faulder, 1794–8) from the end of the eighteenth century, treated

it as authentic. Later it was accepted and frequently repeated, probably as a part explanation of what one regarded as his 'extraordinary' career. According to the *Biographia Navalis* he was a lieutenant in Sir John Narborough's squadron in 1674, and distinguished himself in the fight against the Tripoli Corsairs by burning the Dey's ships in the harbour. In the same year he was made captain of a fifth-rate. Like many other tarpaulin commanders he disagreed with the policy of James II and made little further progress in his career before 1688. He distinguished himself in the Battle of Bantry Bay, and was knighted shortly after by William of Orange. At the battle of La Hogue, he was the first to break through the enemy line, [and] was put in joint command of the fleet with Admiral Killigrew and Sir Ralph Delaval. In 1705, he was Commander-in-Chief of the British fleets. In 1707, on his return from the unsuccessful attempt on Toulon, he was shipwrecked and drowned near the Scilly Islands. His wife was the widow of his old chief and protector, Sir John Narborough. His daughter married Lord Romney.

31 Under 13 January 1666, Pepys wrote in his diary: 'His (Myngs's) father being always and at this day a shoemaker and his mother a hoyman's daughter of which he was frequently to boast.' The *DNB* adds that 'this statement is certainly exaggerated, if not entirely false. His parents were of well-to-do families in the North of Norfolk. His father . . . seems to have been a near kinsman if not a son of Nicholas Mynnes, the representative of a good old Norfolk family. His mother, Katherine Parr, was the daughter of Christopher Parr, the owner of property.'

Controversies of this type, particularly with regard to the seamen commanders of the sixteenth and seventeenth centuries, can be found frequently enough in naval biographies. It may be said, therefore, that stock phrases like 'good family' or 'owner of property' help comparatively little towards elucidating the social status of a family unless they are accompanied by a more detailed statement of the size and character of this property, of the occupation of its owner and above all of the social status accorded to a man and his family by his contemporaries. For whatever our opinion may be, a seventeenth-century family was a 'good family' only if it was regarded as such by its contemporaries.

In that respect, there can be little doubt about the status of Sir Christopher Myngs. In his own time he was always regarded as a man of common descent. In the navy he was known as one of the tarpaulin commanders. He was actually one of the few tarpaulins who remained in favour after the Restoration. In 1664 he hoisted his flag as vice-admiral of a Channel squadron; he was knighted in 1665; but at his funeral in 1666, as Pepys noted, no person of quality was present with the exception of Sir William Coventry.

32 1665–7. – eds.

33 Charnock, *Biographia Navalis*, II, p. 105.

34 *Biographia Britannica*, 6 vols (London: W. Innys, 1747–66), I, p. 179.

35 *DNB*.

36 Campbell, *Lives of the British Admirals*, IV, p. 233: 'in King Charles II's reign he was owner and commander of a ship called the Benbow Frigate. . . . He was always considered by the merchants as a bold, brave and active commander. . . . no man was better . . . respected by the merchants upon the Exchange than Captain Benbow. . . . The diligence and activity of Captain Benbow could not fail of recommending him to the favour of . . . King William to whose personal kindness founded on a just sense of Benbow's merit he owed his being so early promoted to a flag.'

37 Ibid., p. 234.

38 Campbell, *Lives of the British Admirals*, vol. I.

39 Charnock, *Biographia Navalis*, II, p. 35.

40 Named after his maternal grandfather, Sir Henry Winston of Standiston. Winston Churchill, knighted in 1663, was afterwards Commissioner of the Court of Claims in Ireland and one of the Clerk Comptrollers of the Green-Cloth.

41 Gentleman of the long robe: lawyer. – eds.

42 Campbell, *Lives of the British Admirals*, III, pp. 279 f.

43 A century later, from the second half of the eighteenth century on, the status of a gentleman was accorded to clergymen, and to their sons, more or less as a matter of course. In the seventeenth and the early eighteenth centuries professional training and professional functions alone did not confer on people the status of a gentleman. The higher clergy, especially the bishops, ranked as gentlemen because these positions were usually reserved for people born into the gentleman classes. The poorer clergy ranked with craftsmen, tradesmen and workmen because they mostly came from, and lived like, the common people. And other occupations which we call professions, for instance that of lawyers, were equally divided; they did not form part of what later generations came to call the 'professional middle classes'. As for the naval profession, anomalous in its conditions was not so

much the fact that it recruited itself from different sections of society, but rather the fact that men from the lower sections could occupy the same positions and rise to the same ranks as those from the higher.

44 Pepys, *Tangier Papers*, p. 121.

45 Monson, *Naval Tracts*, vol. I.

46 R. Gibson left a list of all tarpaulin commanders who from the time of Elizabeth up to his own time became flag officers. Apparently, his list does not include tarpaulin commanders who became flag officers under William III. Gibson mentions six admirals, nine vice-admirals and four rear admirals (Charnock, *History of Marine Architecture*, vol. I, p. xc). It seems reasonable to assume that among captains, masters and commanders etc. the proportion of professional seamen was usually greater than among admirals.

47 In 1950, when this essay was first published, the post-war Labour government had recently nationalised various major British industries. The British Transport Commission for instance was headed by a former senior civil servant, Cyril Hurcomb (1883–1975), while the chairman of the Central Electricity Generating Board was the leading trade unionist Walter Citrine (1887–1983); both were made members of the House of Lords. – eds

48 This is a recurrent theme in Elias's thinking, from his discussion of the changing structure of the early modern French upper classes in *The Civilising Process* [*On the Process of Civilisation*, Collected Works, vol. 3] and *The Court Society* [Collected Works, vol. 2] to his study of working-class groups in *The Established and the Outsiders* [Collected Works, vol. 4]. – eds.

49 Pepys, *Tangier Papers*, p. 122.

50 George Savile, Marquis of Halifax, *A Rough Draught of a New Model at Sea* (London: Banks, 1694), p. 7.

51 Ibid., p. 22.

2
Tensions and Conflicts

The source for the introductory section and the section on the formative conflict, Drake and Doughty, is NE Archive 507; source for the subsequent sections 3–6 is NE Archive 508.

1 See note on 'Gentlemen and tarpaulin commanders', in H. Mainwaring, *The Life and Works of Sir Henry Mainwaring*, ed. G. E. Manwaring and

W. G. Perrin (London: Navy Records Society, 1922) vol. II [Pub. NRS, vol. 56], pp. 279–81 (apparently written *c.*1623, first edition [?] 1644, another edition 1670).

2   The more one tries to understand not only social structures (e.g. class structures) but also social relationships, the less satisfactory does it seem to make general statements without presenting at the same time representative samples of the concrete situations from which they have been abstracted. The finding of recurrent regularities may be the aim of these studies, but these regularities remain inevitably somewhat vague, however precise the manner of their presentation, if they are expressed alone in a general and abstract form. The presentation of life situations in social studies poses a number of problems. Without it they are incomplete.

3   [The text published in Dutch translation in *De Gids* starts here.] More details on the composition of Drake's fleet are found in N. M. Penzer (ed.) *The World Encompassed* (London: Argonaut Press, 1926); on p. 142, Cooke's narrative begins: 'The XV Novembar in the yere above written [AD 1577] Francys Drake, John Winter, and Thomas Doughty, as eqwall companyons and frindly gentlemen with a fleett of fyve ships and to the numbar of 164 gentlemen and saylers departed Plimouthe.'

4   E. G. R. Taylor, 'More light on Drake', *Mariner's Mirror* XVI (1930), pp. 134–51; E. G. R. Taylor, 'Master John Dee, Drake and the Straits of Anian', *Mariner's Mirror* XV (1929), pp. 125–30. [Largely reprinted in Taylor, *Tudor Geography* (London: Methuen, 1930) pp. 113–19. – eds].

5   Drake came, it seems, from peasant stock. His father, Edmund Drake, was the younger son of a family of tenants on Lord Russell's Bedford estate. By profession Edmund Drake had been a sailor; he had, like many other seamen of his time, embraced a Protestant creed of a strongly sectarian and revivalist brand. For a short time after his marriage he had settled down to a landsman's life in a cottage on Lord Russell's estate. But when the peasantry of Devonshire, still predominantly Catholic at that time, rose in revolt against the introduction of Cranmer's Prayer Book by Somerset, he and his family were driven out of their cottage and had to flee for their lives. They found a refuge at the Medway where Edmund Drake made a living as a Bible reader to the fleet. They lived poorly enough in a disused hulk. There Francis Drake grew up. His father taught him what little book learning he had. 'My bringing up', he said later (Penzer (ed.), *World Encompassed*, p. 163), 'has not been in learning'. He could certainly read; he could write,

though rather slowly and not without difficulties. He was still a boy when his father apprenticed him to the owner and captain of a small bark engaged in the coasting trade. He had, in short, as one of his biographers wrote (A. E. W. Mason, *The Life of Francis Drake* (London: Hodder & Stoughton, 1941), p. 5) a 'hard and bitter schooling.'

From these humble beginnings he rose largely as a result of his own efforts and talents. As captain and owner of merchantmen he acquired some wealth. His fame spread thanks to his exploits as privateer. When he became, in 1577, the leader of an expedition sponsored by the Queen and members of the Privy Council, he had climbed higher than ever before. And he certainly meant to live up to his new station. He made 'provisions for ornament and delight', carrying with him for this purpose 'expert musicians and rich furniture' (Penzer (ed.), *World Encompassed*, p. 2). He was served 'on silver dishes with gold borders and gilded garlands in which were his arms'. He carried with him 'all possible dainties and perfumed waters', explaining that many of these had been given to him by the Queen (ibid., p. 215). In short he saw himself in the role of a great gentleman. However, although it was possible for Drake to be accepted, at least outwardly, by other gentlemen as their equal, throughout his live he suffered from disabilities characteristic of social rise. Later generations tended to think more of the man and his personal achievements. His social status became a matter of small importance. His contemporaries never lost sight of it. The Queen could make him an admiral and later a knight. Many of her courtiers probably never ceased to regard him as an upstart. It could happen that a soldier openly expressed his disgust at the idea of serving under Drake (J. S. Corbett, *Drake and the Tudor Navy, With a History of the Rise of England as a Maritime Power* (London: Longmans, Green & Co., 1898), I, p. 236). At the end of the century Sir Fulke Greville, in his *Life of Sir Philip Sidney* (London, 1652, written *c.*1595), p. 84, still spoke of him as a 'mean born subject of her Majesty the Queen'.

6   Robert Dudley, Earl of Leicester (1532–88), favourite of Queen Elizabeth. – eds.

7   Sir Francis Walsingham (1530–90), Lord Privy Seal – principal secretary – to Queen Elizabeth 1576–90, and her intelligence and security chief. – eds.

8   The post of Lord High Admiral was one of the nine 'great offices of state'; at this time it was held by Edward Fiennes Clinton, Earl of Lincoln (1512–85), who took a stake in Drake's expedition. – eds.

9 J. A. Williamson, *The Age of Drake* (London: Adam & Charles Black, 1946), p. 168.

10 Doughty's version apparently was, as some witnesses later reported, that he and Drake conferred about the voyage together in Ireland 'to do it of themselves', that he, Thomas Doughty, 'went to Mr Secretary Walsingham and to Mr Hatton and like a true subject broke the matter to them and they broke it to the Queen's Majesty who had great good liking of it and caused our Captain (Drake) to be sent for' (Penzer (ed.), *World Encompassed*, p. 158). Drake himself said that he owed his introduction to Hawkins.

11 This term, which accurately describes Drake's concept of his own position as leader of this expedition, was used explicitly, it seems, by Drake himself on a later occasion when he again became involved in a struggle for leadership with a gentleman.

When he helped to prepare the defences against the coming of the Spanish Armada, he at first took it almost for granted that the Queen would appoint him as Commander-in-Chief of her Navy in preference to Lord Howard; and although he suffered a setback on that occasion and had to be content with the position of Lord Howard's second-in-command, he stood back, in obedience to the Queen's orders, with undisguised reluctance and not without stressing his great moderation and self-restraint in doing so.

'He had looked', as a contemporary historian wrote (Ubaldino, quoted in Corbett, *Drake and the Tudor Navy*, II, p. 153), 'to being appointed as admiral in absolute command of that enterprise, as being a man belike thought fatal to the Spaniards. Yet though it must have been so, respect being had only to his merit and his known good fortune hitherto, still at the same time at Court, it had to be taken into consideration that since intelligence had been received how the Spanish Armada was to have at his head the Duke of Medina-Sidonia, a prince of great consequence in those realms, they should have also to put forward against him a man of noble and illustrious family . . . All which things being well pondered and considered by Sir Francis Drake, in setting an example of singular self-restraint, he rendered vain all fears which had been felt about the uncertainty of their acting together.' This passage, as Corbett said, gives perhaps the clearest insight into Drake's character that we possess. It also sheds some light on his attitude towards his less exalted rival on his voyage round the world.

12 J. D. Upcott, *Three Voyages of Drake as recorded in contemporary records* (London: Ginn, 1936), p. 5, n. 1.

13 Penzer (ed.), *World Encompassed*, p. 146.

14 Corbett, *Drake and the Tudor Navy*, I, p. 234.

15 'Certain speeches used by Thomas Doughty aboard of the Flyboat in the hearing of me, John Sarocold, and others', Vaux (ed.), *World Encompassed*, pp. 166–74.

Drake's former friend has often been represented as the villain of the piece, scheming against Drake's rightful authority and stirring up trouble, simply because he was by nature a bad character and a traitor. One of the worst actions traditionally held against him was an alleged intrigue against the Earl of Essex. All that is really known about this matter, however, is the fact that Essex himself believed, or professed to believe, that Doughty had been disloyal to him. In the same way, Hawkins believed at one time (after the action at the Mexican port of San Juan d'Ulloa in 1568) that Drake had been disloyal. With a little diligence one might find other similar incidents in Drake's life or, for that matter, in that of many other famous men of that time. One sometimes has the impression that in those days the capacity both for being loyal and for being disloyal was greater than it is today. However, the more human, and the tragic, aspects of this as of so many other conflicts between people come to light only if one considers fairly the situation in which both sides found themselves, their group situation, and the feeling experienced by both in relation to each other. Doughty, whatever else he may have been, was by upbringing a gentleman. He represented a type of soldier fairly new at that time; he could not only fight, but he also had considerable learning and culture. He had studied law. He knew Greek and some Hebrew. He had lived in close contact with some of the greatest men at court. One can assume that in manner and dress, he was a courtier as well as a soldier. If Doughty's enemies, and particularly Drake, came to regard him as a traitor, other friends apparently held him in high esteem and liked him well.

'His qualities in a man of his time', wrote one of them (Penzer (ed.), *World Encompassed*, p. 125), 'were rare and his gifts very excellent for his age, a sweet orator, a pregnant philosopher, a good gift for the Greek tongue and a reasonable taste of Hebrew, a sufficient Secretary to a noble personage of great place and in Ireland an approved soldier and not behind many in the study of the law for his time . . . he was delighted in the study, hearing and practice of the word of God, daily exercising himself by reading, meditating to himself, conferring with others, instructing of the ignorant, as if he had been a minister of Christ . . .'.

147

16 That others shared his opinions is borne out by John Cooke's narrative (Penzer (ed.), *World Encompassed*, p. 142).

17 Ibid., pp. 150–1.

18 Ibid., p. 149.

19 Ibid., p. 157.

20 Elias later used Gregory Bateson's term 'double bind' to characterise such processes; see *Involvement and Detachment* (Dublin: UCD Press, 2007 [Collected Works, vol. 8]), p. 108. – eds.

21 Cooke's narrative, Penzer (ed.), *World Encompassed*, p. 155.

22 Nuno da Silva's statement, translated in Z. Nuttall (ed.), *New Light on Drake: A Collection of Documents Relating to His Voyage of Circumnavigation 1577–1580* (London: Hakluyt Society, 2nd series, no. 34, 1914), p. xlix.

23 Cooke's narrative, Penzer (ed.), *World Encompassed*, p. 158: 'Whether he forgot his commission or not, truly I think it should have been shown to the uttermost, if he had had it.'

24 Ibid., p. 206.

25 Elias was experimenting with different endings for 'Drake and Doughty'. The article in *De Gids* ends at this point, but the typescript continues and concludes with the famous 'haul and draw' quotation from Drake. – eds.

26 Penzer (ed.), *World Encompassed*, p. 164.

27 'The sea', wrote Pepys in 1683, 'can never be a trade for a nobleman or courtier, because it is impossible for him to live so in it but that his conversation and company and diet and clothes and all must be common with the meanest seaman, and his greatest trust too, while his other companions of his own are but trouble to him and no use. Nor can he be neat and nice to make love in the fashion, when he comes among the ladies.' Miscellaneous Notes, in Samuel Pepys, *The Tangier Papers* (London: Navy Records Society [Pub. NRS, vol. 73], 1935), p. 166.

28 'whosoever . . . can live idly and without manuall labour and will beare the port, charge and countenaunce of a gentleman, he shall be called master, for that is the title which men give to esquires and other gentlemen' (T. Smith, *De Republica Anglorum* [1583], ed. L. Alston (Cambridge: Cambridge University Press, 1906), p. 40).

29 There are many other instances showing how jealous the seamen were of the power and status they derived from their special knowledge and skill. When it came to that, they were no less opposed than the gentlemen to

innovations, however useful, which seemed to lessen their power or their traditional privileges. See for example the opposition of the Masters of Trinity House against the 'projected erection of light houses on the North and South Foreland for avoiding the dangers of the Godwin Sands'. *Cal. S. P. Dom.*, 9 Aug., 1634, and 2 Feb. and 25 March, 1635:

> The lights on the South Foreland will be of no service to persons on the Sea, they having marks more certain than lights

and

> there is no necessity for such lighthouses, neither will they be of use which is also the opinion of the masters of the Royal Navy who are the principal pilots of the Kingdom, and are directly against erecting any such lighthouse.'

Compare also their protest against the building of greater ships, *Cal. S. P. Dom.* 9 Aug. 1634: 'The art and wit of man cannot build a ship fit for service with three tier of ordnance.'

30 J. Smith, *An Accidence for the Sea, Very Necessary for all Young Seamen . . . Shewing the Phrases Offices, and Words of Command Belonging to the Building, Rigging and Sayling a Man of Warre, and how to Manage a Navy and a Fight at Sea, etc.* (London: Benjamin Fisher, 1636), p. 54.

31 *The Seaman's Dictionary*, in Mainwaring, *Life and Works*, II, p. 280. *The Seaman's Dictionary* and *An Accidence for the Sea* are two of the little manuals written during the first half of the seventeenth century mainly for the use of gentlemen who wished to acquire quickly from books the knowledge which seamen acquired slowly by years of hard practice. There they could get an idea of their own duties as captains, lieutenants or volunteers as well as of those of masters, boatswains, gunners, carpenters and other seamen. They could learn the names of different parts of the ship. They were instructed about the words of command peculiar to the seafaring community and, generally, unknown to gentlemen, 'it being so', as the author of the *Seaman's Dictionary* wrote, 'that very few gentlemen (though they be called seamen) do fully understand what belongs to their profession'. Another of these handbooks partly identical with *An Accidence for the Sea*, is Captain John Smith's *A Sea Grammar* (London: Printed by Iohn Hauiland, 1627). An excerpt from chap XIII, 'How to manage a fight at sea

with the proper terms', may give an idea as to what gentlemen had to learn: 'Boy fetch my Cellar of Bottels, a Health to you all fore and aft, courage my hearts for a fresh Charge. Gunners, beat open the Ports and out with your lower Tire, and bring me from the weather side to the Lee, so many Pieces as we have Ports to bear upon him. Master, lay him aboard Loufe for Loufe, Midship men, see the Tops and Yards well manned with Stones, Fire-pots and Brass-bails to throw amongst them before we enter, or if we be put off charge them with all your great and small shot; in the smoke let us enter them in the Shrowds, and every Squadron at his best advantage; so, sound Drums and Trumpets and St George for England.'

32 In this section, Elias makes implicit use of his concept of the 'royal mechanism'; see the editors' Introduction, pp. 15–17 above.

33 See for example Corbett, *Drake and the Tudor Navy*, II, p. 155. Henry VIII's Admiral [was expected to] act on general policy discussed and approved by the captains in conclave. The old practice had been for every captain to have a voice. Howard reduced the meeting to seven besides himself: Drake, Lord Thomas Howard, Lord Sheffield, Sir Roger Williams, [John] Hawkins, [Martin] Frobisher and Thomas Fenner. It was a skilful choice, representing all interests. Fenner was one of Drake's men prominent in 1587. The two lords stood for the court interest and Howard's own connections (Sheffield was his son-in-law). Williams was a soldier of repute and was actually called for land service before the fighting began. Hawkins, like Howard himself, represented the Navy Board. Frobisher must have been included on his merits as a good seaman and tried commander, and perhaps in special sympathy with the mariners of the mercantile marine. And under Howard's guidance these men did pull together, although they were not all friends.

34 Missing note [L.P. (Henry VIII) XII, pt. 1, Nos 636, 667 (see also No. 1118) – eds.]

35 Nathaniel Boteler, *Boteler's Dialogues*, ed. W. G. Perrin (London: Navy Records Society, 1929 [Pub. NRS, vol. 65]), p. 6. [The phrase in square brackets that completes the paragraph was omitted by Elias.]

36 Missing note. [Probably intended to refer to Elias's discussion of the formation in the early modern period of a new upper class from people of diverse social origins in Western European countries, in *The Civilising Process* (Oxford: Blackwell, 2000 [*On the Process of Civilisation*, Collected Works, vol. 3]), p. 68 and *passim*. Also relevant are *The Court Society* (Dublin:

UCD Press, 2006 [Collected Works, vol. 2]), and his discussion of the English ruling class in his Introduction to *Quest for Excitement* (Dublin: UCD Press, 2007 [Collected Works, vol. 7]), although neither of those books had been published when Elias wrote his naval essays. – eds.]

37 Missing note. [Edward Hyde, Earl of Clarendon, *The History of the Rebellion and Civil Wars in England*, ed. W. Dunn Macray (Oxford: Clarendon Press, 1888), Book v, §§376–83. – eds.]

3
The Development of the Midshipman

The source for this chapter is NE Archive 513; see the editors' Introduction, p. 19–20 above, for further details.

1   It seems that rather late in the eighteenth century the social qualification of 'gentlemen' is explicitly mentioned in regulations. W. James, *The Naval History of Great Britain* (1st edn, London: Richard Bentley, 1822–4), I, p. 231, apparently quoting the Order in Council of 16 April 1794, speaks of 'young gentlemen volunteers'. It seems that, as a result of this order, only young volunteers could be mustered as 'boys' or volunteers of different kinds instead of as captain's servants. This order, according to James, directed that one fifth of these boys should consist of young gentlemen volunteers, intended for officers. The second class were to keep watch with the seamen, and the remainder were intended chiefly to wait upon the lieutenants and other officers. Thus a differentiation of functions corresponding to differences of birth and upbringing, which had developed primarily by usage in the naval service itself, was regulated by order.

2   W. Falconer, 'The Midshipman', in W. Falconer, *The Shipwreck: And Other Poems* (London: Whittingham, 1822 [1762]):

In canvassed Birth [*sic*] profoundly deap in thought
His busy mind with Sines and Tangents fraught
A Mid reclines! – in calculations lost!

3   Ibid.,

In cheering Grog the rapid course goes round
And not a care in all the circle's found

Promotion, Mess-Debts, absent Friends and Love
Inspired by Hope, in turn their topic prove
To proud superior then they each look up
and curse all discipline in ample cup.

4 Ibid.

5 W. Falconer, *An Universal Dictionary of the Marine*, 3rd edn, rev. J. W. Norie (London: J. Badcock, 1815).

6 Edward Thompson, *Sailor's Letters* (London: T. Becket and P. A. de Hondt, W. Flexney and J. Moran, 1766), I, pp. 142, 144.

7 In 1750 there were still captains and even lieutenants in the navy who had received their commission in the last decade of the seventeenth century.

8 See for example Barnett's letter to Anson quoted in H. W. Richmond, *The Navy in the War of 1739–48* (Cambridge: Cambridge University Press, 1920), I, p. xii: 'I am stupid enough to think that we are worse officers though better seamen than our neighbours. Our young men get wrong notions early, and are led to imagine that he is the greatest officer who has the least blocks in his rigging. I hope you will give a new turn to our affairs and form a society for the propagation of sea-military knowledge. I think you had formerly such a scheme.'

4
Achieving Maritime Supremacy

The source for this chapter is NE Archive 504.

1 W. Monson, *The Naval Tracts of Sir William Monson in Six Books*, ed. M. Oppenheim, 5 vols (London: Navy Records Society, 1913 [Pub. NRS, vol. 45]), IV, p. 63.

2 J. Sarrazin, in Maréchal de camp René-Martin Pillet, *Tableau de la Grande-Bretagne, ou observations sur l'Angleterre, vue à Londres et dans ses provinces... avec un supplement par M. Sarrazin.* Paris: Didot, 1816, p. 200. [Jean Sarrazin (1770–1848), French general (not Field Marshal), who wrote the first overall history of the Peninsular War. – eds.]

3 This translation is by Elias himself (NE-Archive: cover 515); the word *boudeur* might perhaps better be rendered 'sullen' or 'sulky' than 'supercilious'. – eds.

4 Samuel Pepys, *The Tangier Papers*, ed. . . . Edwin Chappell (London: Navy Records Society, 1935 [Pub. NRS, vol. 73]), p. 168.

5 Michael Oppenheim, Introduction to Monson, *Naval Tracts*, I, p. 43.

6 That is to say, at the time of the Battle of Trafalgar as much as at the time of the Armada. – eds.

7 See Elias, *The Court Society* (Dublin: UCD Press, 2006 [Collected Works, vol. 2]), especially Appendix I, 'On the notion that there can be a state without structural conflicts', pp. 294–302. – eds.

8 Jean-Baptiste Colbert (1619–83), Contrôleur Général des Finances (Minister of Finance) under Louis XIV from 1661 and Intendant de la Marine (Navy Minister) from 1663 until his death. The *Code des armées navales* that he had prepared was published only in 1689, after his death. – eds.

9 *Code des armées navales*, Livre VII, Art. I: 'Le choix des Gardes de la Marine sera fait par sa Majesté ou, suivant les ordres qu'elle fera adresser aux intendans dans les Provinces. Il n'en sera reçû aucun s'il n'est Gentilhomme, et sera par eux rapporté des certificats de leur Noblesse, signés des Intendans qui auront commis à cet effet'. [The choice of Marine Guards will be made by His Majesty, following the orders he will give to the Provincial Intendants. None but gentlemen will be received, and they should hold certificates confirming their nobility, which should be signed by the Intendants, who are commissioned to do so. – trans. eds.]

10 René Duguay-Trouin (1673–1736), born into a sailor's family in Saint-Malo, joined the crew of a privateer at 16, became captain of a naval frigate at 24. He won a series of victories over the English and Dutch, and most famously over the Portuguese at Rio de Janeiro in 1711. He was ennobled in 1709. – eds.

11 Jean Bart (1650–1702) was born at Dunkirk into a poor family of sailors. He joined the Dutch navy as a teenager, fighting against the English under the command of Admiral De Ruyter and learning seamanship and naval tactics. In 1672, when war broke out between France and the Netherlands, he returned to France to serve as a privateer. Under Colbert, he was given command of his own ship in 1674, and in 1696 Louis XIV put him in command of the royal fleet. – eds.

12 For a fuller account of this system, Elias here referred the reader to the original German edition of his *Über den Prozess der Zivilisation: Soziogenetische und psychogenetische Untersuchungen* (Basel: Haus zum Falken, 1939) II, p. 150 ff. That corresponds to pp. 272–7 in the revised English edition of

The Civilising Process (Oxford: Blackwell, 2000 [*On the Process of Civilisation*, Collected Works, vol. 3]), and consists of the latter part of his discussion of the 'monopoly mechanism'. In fact, however, his discussion of the 'royal mechanism', pp. 320–8 in the revised English edition, is more relevant to the point he is making here. – eds.

13 L. de Saint Croix, *Essai sur l'histoire de l'administration de la Marine de France*, 1689–1789 (Paris: Calmann Lévy, 1892), p. 13. [trans. eds.]

14 Pepys, *Tangier Papers*, p. 246.

15 See Elias, *Court Society*, esp. pp. 286–93. – eds.

5

The Growing Costs of the Naval Establishment

The source for this chapter is NE Archive 516.

1 F. C. Dietz, *English Public Finance 1558–1641* (New York: Century, 1932), pp. 440–1.

2 See Elias, *The Germans* (Cambridge: Polity, 1996 [*Studies on the Germans*, Collected Works, vol. 11]). – eds.

3 A. J. Griffiths, *Observations on Some Points of Seamanship; With Practical Hints on Naval Economy, etc.* (Cheltenham: J. J. Hadley, 1824), p. 32

4 See Appendix to this chapter, p. 128. – eds.

5 13 George II, c.3.

6 In 1770, by 11 George III, c.3, merchant ships were allowed to have three-quarters of their crews foreigners till 1 February 1772. Acts permitting the same proportion of foreign seamen were passed in 1776, 1778, 1779, 1780, 1781 and 1782. In 1794 it was enacted (34 George III, c.68) 'for the encouragement of British seamen' that after the expiration of six months from the conclusion of the war, vessels in the foreign, as distinguished from the coasting trade were to have their commanders and three-quarters of their crews British subjects. Even at the end of the nineteenth century the number of foreign seamen employed in British ships was not inconsiderable: 41,590 British sailors and 13,432 foreign sailors were employed in British merchant ships in 1891, 35,020 British and 14,469 foreign sailors in 1896. See Sir Nathaniel Barnaby, *Naval Development in the Nineteenth Century* (Toronto: Linscott, 1904), p. 27.

6
On Institutions

The source used is NE Archive 516.

7
The Last Act

The source used is NE Archive 1525. The fragment presented here is derived from a lengthier outline for a play on Drake and Doughty. The total outline is a sketchy and incomplete draft version. The fragment 'The last act' is valuable because it demonstrates deep psychological understanding of the relationship between Drake and Doughty – a relationship that ended dramatically in the decapitation of Doughty. – eds.

Bibliography

PRIMARY SOURCES

SOURCES FROM THE INVENTORY OF THE
NORBERT ELIAS ARCHIVE, PART I

Note: Part I of the catalogue of Elias's papers in the Deutsche Literaturarchiv, Marbach am Neckar, is the main listing, but the supplementary catalogue NAVAL contains scraps and duplicates.

503   Text of outline of 'The genesis of the naval profession'. n.d. 1 folder.

504   Manuscript with note with heading 'Comparative development in France and Spain', pp. 11–34, incomplete. n.d. 1 folder.

505   Manuscript with note with heading 'Copies of development in France and Spain and beginnings in England', pp. 13–62, incomplete, carbon copy. n.d. 1 folder. See also supplementary catalogue NAVAL, 5.

506   Manuscript of 'Studies in the genesis of the naval profession. 2. The formative conflict', pp. 1–20, largely original with some carbon copies. n.d. 1 folder.

507   Manuscript of 'Studies in the genesis of the naval profession. 2. The formative conflict', pp. 1–13, unfinished. n.d. 1 folder.

508   Manuscript with note with heading 'Growth Henry VIII to Charles I', pp. 14–25. 1955. 1 folder.

509   Manuscript of 'The genesis of the naval profession. Gentlemen into seamen', pp. 1–3, 14–15, 25, incomplete, carbon copy with handwritten corrections. n.d. 1 folder. See also supplementary catalogue NAVAL, 6.

510   Manuscript of 'The genesis of the naval profession. Gentlemen into seamen', pp. 1–22, incomplete, carbon copy with hand-written corrections. n.d. 1 folder. See also supplementary catalogue NAVAL, 7.

511   Manuscript of 'The genesis of the naval profession. Gentlemen into seamen', pp. 1–2, incomplete, carbon copy. n.d. 1 folder.

512　Manuscript of 'Naval Officers in the nineteenth century. An occupational study. I. The genesis of an occupation', pp. 1–6e, incomplete. n.d. 1 folder. See also supplementary catalogue NAVAL, 8.

513　Manuscript with note with heading 'Development of midshipman with French comparison', pp. 7–17, version with mark A, incomplete. n.d. 1 folder. See also supplementary catalogue NAVAL, 9.

514　Manuscript with note with heading 'Continuation to Drake rivalry. (1) Captain – master (2) Master – lieutenant', pp. 1–16, version with mark B. n.d. 1 folder. See also supplementary catalogue NAVAL, 10.

515　Text of 'A Study in Tensions', several concepts of beginnings, versions with marks Q and O. n.d. 1 folder.

516　Manuscript with note with heading 'Growing costs of naval establishment. Comparison Elizabeth and Cromwell etc.', pp. 9–16, largely original with some carbon copies, incomplete, with additonal notes. n.d. 1 folder.

517　File concerning 'Studies in the Genesis of the Naval Profession', with numbered pages belonging to several manuscripts. n.d. 1 folder. See also supplementary catalogue NAVAL, 1.

518　File concerning manuscripts of 'Studies in the Genesis of the Naval Profession', with notes, unnumbered pages and newspaper clippings. n.d. 1 folder.

525　Text by N. Elias of an outline of a play on Drake and Doughty, with annexes. n.d. 1 folder.

　　　MISC-D X = Paris 3: Transcription de l'éxposé présenté par Norbert Elias au Colloque Historique Franco-allemand, en date du 17 mars '83

SECONDARY SOURCES

WORKS TO WHICH ELIAS MAKES REFERENCE

Boteler, Nathaniel, *Boteler's Dialogues*, ed. W.G. Perrin (London: Navy Records Society, 1929 [Pub. NRS, vol. 65]).

Barlow, E., *Barlow's Journal of his Life at Sea in King's Ships, East & West Indiamen & other Merchantmen from 1659 to 1703*, transcribed from the original manuscript by Basil Lubbock, 2 vols (London: Hurst & Blackett, 1934).

Barnaby, N., *Naval Development in the Nineteenth Century* (Toronto and Philadelphia: Linscott; London and Edinburgh: W. & R. Chambers, 1904).

Biographia Britannica, 6 vols (London: W. Innys, 1747–66).

Campbell, J., *Lives of the British Admirals, Containing also a New and Accurate Naval History, from the Earliest Periods*, 4 vols (London: J. & H. Pemberton, T. Waller, 1742–4). [Enlarged edn, 8 vols, continued to the year 1779 by Dr Berkenhout (London: C. & J. Barrington, J. Harris, 1812)].

Carr-Saunders, A. M. and P. A. Wilson, *The Professions* (Oxford: Clarendon Press, 1933).

Charnock, John, *Biographia Navalis*, 6 vols (London: R. Faulder, 1794–8).

Charnock, John, *An History of Marine Architecture*, 3 vols (London: R. Faulder, &c. 1800–2)

Clarendon, Edward Hyde, Earl of, *The History of the Rebellion and Civil Wars in England*, ed. W. Dunn Macray (Oxford: Clarendon Press, 1888).

Clowes, W. L., *The Royal Navy: A History from the Earliest Times to the Present* (London: Sampson Low, Marston, 1898).

Colbert, Jean-Baptiste (attr. to), *Ordonnance pour les armées navales et arcenaux de marine (15 avril 1689)*, Paris, 1689.

Corbett, Julian S., *Drake and the Tudor Navy: With a History of the Rise of England as a Maritime Power*, 2 vols (London: Longmans, Green, 1898).

Cremer, John, *Ramblin' Jack, the Journal of Captain John Cremer, 1700–1774*, transcribed by R. Reynell Bellamy (London: Jonathan Cape, 1936).

Dictionary of National Biography, ed. Leslie Stephen and Sidney Lee, 63 vols (London: Smith, Elder, 1885–1900).

D'Ewes, Simonds, *The Journal of Sir Simonds D'Ewes: from the First Recess of the Long Parliament to the Withdrawal of King Charles from London*, ed. Willson Havelock Coates (New Haven, CT: Yale University Press, 1942).

Dietz, F.C., *English Public Finance 1558–1641* (New York: Century, 1932).

Elias, Norbert, *Über den Prozess der Zivilisation: Soziogenetische und psychogenetische Untersuchungen*, 2 vols (Basel: Haus zum Falken, 1939). [English translation: *The Civilising Process* (rev. edn Oxford: Blackwell, 2000 [*On the Process of Civilisation*, Collected Works, vol. 3])]

Falconer, W., 'The Midshipman', in Falconer, *The Shipwreck: And Other Poems* (London: Whittingham, 1822 [1762]).

Falconer, W., *An Universal Dictionary of the Marine*, 3rd edn revised, corrected and improved by J. W. Norie (London: T. Cadell and W. Daviesand J. Murray, 1815 [1769]).

Ginsberg, M., 'The work of L. T. Hobhouse', in J. A. Hobson and M. Ginsberg (eds), *L. T. Hobhouse: His Life and Work* (London: Allen & Unwin, 1931).

Greville, Fulke, *Life of Sir Philip Sidney*, with an introduction by Nowell Smith (Oxford: Clarendon Press, 1907) [originally published 1652, written c.1595].

Griffiths, A. J., *Observations on Some Points of Seamanship; With Practical Hints on Naval Economy, etc.* (Cheltenham: J. J. Hadley, 1824).

Hunter, Sir William Wilson, *History of British India*, 2 vols (London: Longmans, Green, 1899–1900).

James, W., *The Naval History of Great Britain*, 5 vols (London: Richard Bentley, 1822).

Laughton, Sir John Knox (ed.), *Naval Miscellany*, vol II (London: Navy Records Society, 1912 [Pub. NRS, vol. 40])

Laughton, Sir John Knox, 'Historians and naval history', in Julian S. Corbett and H. J. Edwards, (eds), *Naval and Military Essays* (Cambridge: Cambridge University Press, 1914), pp. 3–22.

Mainwaring, Henry *The Life and Works of Sir Henry Mainwaring*, ed. G. E. Manwaring [vol. II with W. G. Perrin], 2 vols (London: Navy Records Society, 1920–22 [Pub. NRS, vols 54, 56]).

Mason, A. E. W., *The Life of Francis Drake* (London: Hodder & Stoughton, 1941).

Menen, A., *The Prevalence of Witches* (London: Chatto & Windus, 1947).

Monson, William, *The Naval Tracts of Sir William Monson in Six Books*, ed. Michael Oppenheim (5 vols, London: Navy Records Society, 1902–14 [Pub. NRS, vols 22, 23, 43, 45, 47]).

Nuttall, Zelia (ed.), *New Light on Drake: A Collection of Documents Relating to His Voyage of Circumnavigation 1577–1580* (London: Hakluyt Society, 1914).

Penn, Granville, *Memorials of the Professional Life and Times of Sir William Penn, Admiral and General of the Fleet, during the Interregnum; Admiral, and Commissioner of the Admiralty and Navy after the Restoration: from 1644 to 1670*, 2 vols (London: Duncan, 1833).

Penzer, N. M. (ed.), *The World Encompassed and Analogous Contemporary Documents concerning Sir Francis Drake's Circumnavigation of the World* (London: Argonaut Press, 1926).

Pepys, Samuel, *Naval Minutes*, ed. J. R. Tanner (London: Navy Records Society, 1926 [Pub. NRS, vol. 60])

Pepys, Samuel, *The Tangier Papers*, transcr., ed. and collated with the transcription of Mr. W. Matthews by Edwin Chappell (London: Navy Records Society, 1935 [Pub. NRS, vol. 73]).

Public Record Office, Great Britain, *Calendar of State Papers, Domestic series* [*Calendar of State Papers Domestic*] (London: various publishers, 1856–).

Public Record Office, Great Britain, *Calendar of State Papers and manuscripts, relating to English affairs, existing in the archives and collections of Venice, and in other libraries of northern Italy* [*Calendar of State Papers Venetian*] (London: various publishers, 1864–1947).

Richmond, H. W., *The Navy in the War of 1739–48*, 3 vols (Cambridge: Cambridge University Press, 1920).

Saint Croix, L. de, *Essay sur l'histoire de l'administration de la Marine de France, 1689–1789* (Paris: Calmann Lévy, 1892).

Sarrazin, J., *supplément*, in Maréchal de camp René-Martin Pillet, *Tableau de la Grande-Bretagne, ou observations sur l'Angleterre, vue à Londres et dans ses provinces... avec un supplement par M. Sarrazin*. Paris: Didot, 1816.

Savile, George, Marquis of Halifax, *A Rough Draught of a New Model at Sea* (London: Banks, 1694).

Smith, John, *The Generall Historie of Virginia, New England & the Summer Isles* (Glasgow: MacLehose, 1907 [1624]).

Smith, John, *A Sea Grammar* (London: Printed by Iohn Hauiland, 1627). [Facsimile edn, Amsterdam: Theatrum Orbis Terrarum and New York: Da Capo Press, 1968.]

Smith, John, *An Accidence for the Sea. Very Necessary for all Young Seamen . . . Shewing the Phrases Offices, and Words of Command Belonging to the Building, Rigging and Sayling a Man of Warre, and how to Manage a Navy and a Fight at Sea, etc.* (London: Benjamin Fisher, 1636).

Smith, John, *The Seaman's Grammar* (London: Andrew Kemb, 1953 [1652]).

Smith, T., *De Republica Anglorum*, ed. L. Alston (Cambridge: Cambridge University Press, 1906 [1583]).

Taylor, E. G. R., 'More Light on Drake', *Mariner's Mirror* XVI (1930), pp. 134–51.

Taylor, E. G. R., 'Master John Dee, Drake and the Straits of Anian', *Mariner's Mirror* XV (1929), pp. 125–30.

Upcott, J. D., *Three Voyages of Drake as Recorded in Contemporary Records* (London: Ginn, 1936).

Vaux, W. S. W. (ed.), *The World Encompassed by Sir Francis Drake* (London: Hakluyt Society, 1856).

Williamson, J. A., *The Age of Drake* (London: Adam & Charles Black, 1946 [1938]).

WORKS TO WHICH EDITORIAL REFERENCE IS MADE

Caforio, G. (ed.), 'The military profession in Europe', *Current Sociology* 42: 3 (1994), pp. 107–29.

Caforio, G. (ed.), *The Sociology of the Military* (Cheltenham: Edward Elgar, 1998).

Capp, B., *Cromwell's Navy* (Oxford: Clarendon Press, 1989).

Dandeker, Christopher, 'From patronage to bureaucratic control: the case of the naval officer in English society 1780–1850', *British Journal of Sociology* 29: 3 (1978), pp. 300–20.

Davies, J. D., *Gentlemen and Tarpaulins: The Officers and Men of the Restoration Navy* (Oxford: Clarendon Press, 1991).

Doorn, J. A. A. van, *Sociologie van de organisatie* (Leiden: Stenfert Kroese, 1956).

Doorn, J. A. A. van, 'The officer corps: a fusion of profession and organisation', *Archives Européennes de Sociologie* 6: 2 (1965), pp. 262–82.

Doorn, J. A. A. van and M. Janowitz (eds), *Armed Forces and Society: Sociological Essays* (The Hague: Mouton, 1968).

Doorn, J. A. A. van and C. J. Lammers, 'Repliek', *Sociologische Gids* 9: 1 (1962), pp. 39–48.

Doorn, J. A. A. van and C. J. Lammers, '*Moderne sociologie*: de bezwarden van Goudsblom', *Amsterdams Sociologisch Tijdschrift* 7: 3 (1980), pp. 339–43.

Durkheim, Émile *The Rules of Sociological Method* (Glencoe, IL: Free Press, 1964 [1895]).

Elias, Norbert, 'Studies in the genesis of the naval profession, 1: gentlemen and tarpaulins'. *British Journal of Sociology* 1: 4 (1950), pp. 291–309.

Elias, Norbert, 'Professions', in Julius Gould and William L. Kolb (eds), *A Dictionary of the Social Sciences* (New York, Free Press, 1964), p. 542.

Elias, Norbert *The Court Society* (Dublin: UCD Press, 2006 [Collected Works, vol. 2]) [Orig. German, 1969].

Elias, Norbert, 'Drake en Doughty: De ontwikkeling van een conflict', trans. Nelleke Fuchs-van Maaren, *De Gids*, 140: 5–6 (1977), pp. 223–37.

Elias, Norbert, *What is Sociology?* (London: Hutchinson, 1978 [Collected Works, vol. 5])

Elias, Norbert, *Reflections on a Life* (Cambridge: Polity, 1994 [*Autobiographical Essays and Interviews*, Collected Works, vol. 17]).

Elias, Norbert, *The Germans: Power Struggles and the Development of Habitus in the Nineteenth and Twentieth Centuries* (Cambridge: Polity, 1996). [*Studies on the Germans*, Collected Works, vol. 11]).

Elias, Norbert, 'Estudos sobre a gênese da profissão naval: cavalheiros e tarpaulins', *Mana* 7: 1 (2001), pp. 89–116. [Studies in the Genesis of the Naval Profession: Gentlemen and Tarpaulins].

Elias, Norbert, 'Etudes sur les origines de la profession de marin', *Les*

Champs de Mars 13: 4 (2003), pp. 7–23 [Studies in the Genesis of the Naval Profession].

Elias, Norbert, *Early Writings* (Dublin: UCD Press, 2006 [Collected Works, vol. 1]).

Elias, Norbert, *The Court Society* (Dublin: UCD Press, 2006 [Collected Works, vol. 2]).

Elias, Norbert, *Involvement and Detachment* (Dublin: UCD Press, 2007 [Collected Works, vol. 8]).

Elias, Norbert and Eric Dunning, *Quest for Excitement: Sport and Leisure in the Civilising Process* (Oxford: Blackwell, 1986 [Collected Works, vol. 7]).

N. Elias and J. L. Scotson, *The Established and the Outsiders: A Sociological Enquiry into Community Problems* (London: Frank Cass, 1965 [Collected Works, vol. 4]).

Goudsblom, Johan, *Sociology in the Balance* (Oxford: Blackwell, 1977).

Goudsblom, Johan, *De sociologie van Norbert Elias*. Amsterdam: Meulenhoff, 1987.

Goudsblom, Johan, 'Een kritiek op *Moderne Sociologie* [by J. van Doorn and C. J. Lammers]', *Sociologische Gids* 9: 1 (1962), pp. 28–39.

Goudsblom, Johan, '*Moderne sociologie*: de systematiek geanalyseerd', *Amsterdams Sociologisch Tijdschrift* 6: 3 (1979), pp. 371–98.

Goudsblom, Johan, 'Nawoord', *Amsterdams Sociologisch Tijdschrift* 7: 3 (1980), pp. 339–43.

Goudsblom, Johan, 'Responses to Norbert Elias's work in England, Germany, the Netherlands and France', in P. R. Gleichmann, J. Goudsblom and H. Korte (eds), *Essays for/Aufsätze für Norbert Elias* (Amsterdam: Stichting Amsterdams Sociologisch Tijdschrift, 1977), pp. 37–99.

Goudsblom, Johan and Mennell, Stephen (eds), *The Norbert Elias Reader: A Biographical Selection* (Oxford: Blackwell, 1998).

Homans, G. C., 'The small warship', *American Sociological Review* 11: 3 (1946), pp. 294–300.

Hurd, Geoffrey (ed.), *Human Societies: An Introduction to Sociology* (London: Routledge & Kegan Paul, 1973).

Janowitz, Morris, *The Professsional Soldier: A Social and Political Portrait* (Glencoe, IL: Free Press, 1960).

Johnson, Terence J., *Professions and Power* (London: Macmillan, 1972).

Kuhlmann, J., *The Present and Future of the Military Profession – Views of European Officers* (Strausberg: Sowi, 1996).

Lammers, C. J., 'Strikes and mutinies: a comparative study of organisational conflicts between rulers and ruled', *Administrative Science Quarterly* 14: 4 (1969), pp. 558–72.

Lewis, M., *England's Sea-officers: The Story of the Naval Profession* (London: George Allen & Unwin, 1939).

Macaulay, Thomas Babington, *The History of England from the Accession of James the Second* (10th edn, London: Longman, Brown, Green, & Longmans, 1854), vol. 1.

Marquand, David, *Decline of the Public* (Cambridge: Polity, 2004).

Mennell, Stephen, *Norbert Elias: Civilisation and the Human Self-Image* (Oxford: Blackwell, 1989). [Rev. edn, *Norbert Elias: An Introduction* (Dublin: UCD Press, 1998).]

Mennell, Stephen, 'Elias and the counter-ego', *History of the Human Sciences* 19: 2 (2006), pp. 73–91.

Moelker, René, 'Méér dan een beroep', in R. Moelker and J. Soeters (eds), *Krijgsmacht en Samenleving: klassieke en eigentijdse inzichten* (Amsterdam: Boom, 2003), pp. 116–50.

Moelker, René, 'Norbert Elias, maritime supremacy and the naval profession: on Elias's unpublished studies in the genesis of the naval profession', *British Journal of Sociology* 54: 3 (2003), pp. 373–90.

Moelker, René, 'The Last Knights', in H. Kirkels, W. Klinkert and R. Moelker (eds), *ARMS 2003 Officer Education: The road to Athens* (Breda: Royal Netherlands Military Academy, 2003).

Padfield, P., *Maritime Supremacy and the Opening of the Western Mind* (London: Pimlico, 2000).

Pepys, Samuel, *The Diary of Samuel Pepys*, ed. Robert Latham and William Matthews, 12 vols (London: Bell & Hyman, 1971).

Rodger, N. A. M., *The Safeguard of the Sea*, vol. 1, 660–1649, of *A Naval History of Britain* (London: HarperCollins and National Maritime Museum, 1997).

Rodger, N. A. M., *The Command of the Ocean*, vol. 2, 1649–1815, of *A Naval History of Britain* (London: Allen Lane and National Maritime Museum, 2004).

Simmel, Georg, *The Sociology of Georg Simmel*, ed. Kurt H. Wolff (Glencoe, IL: Free Press, 1950).

Taylor, E. G. R., *Tudor Geography* (London: Methuen, 1930).

Teitler, G., *Toepassing van geweld* (Meppel: Boom, 1972).

Teitler, G., *De wording van het professionele officierscorps* (Rotterdam: Universitaire Pers Rotterdam, 1974).

Teitler, G., *The Genesis of the Professional Officers' Corps* (London: Sage, 1977).

Tilly, Charles, 'Reflections on the history of European state-making', in Tilly (ed.), *The Formation of National States in Western Europe* (Princeton, NJ: Princeton University Press, 1975), pp. 3–83.

Wouters, Cas, 'Ja, ja, ik was nog niet zoo'n beroerde kerel, die zoo'n vriend had' (Nescio), in Han Israëls, Mieke Komen and Abram de Swaan (eds), *Over Elias* (Amsterdam: Het Spinhuis, 1993) [English translation to be published as appendix 'On Norbert Elias and informalisation theory' to Wouters, *Informalization: Manners and Emotions since 1890* (London: Sage, 2007).]

Index

under Elizabeth I 32, 35, 37, 50,
115, 140n
early Stuart 48, 52, 78
under Charles I 71, 74, 76, 81–5
in civil war 137–8n
under Commonwealth 42, 80,
115–20
Restoration 11, 16–17, 21, 36,
75
under Charles II 11, 21, 42, 46,
78, 142n
under James II 11, 78, 115
under William & Mary 21, 35,
44, 52, 106, 119, 141n,
143n
19th cent. 90
navy, French 12, 13, 17, 79, 81,
92–7
under Louis XIV 13, 103,
105–6, 107, 108
navy, Spanish 2, 3, 12, 14, 15,
92–7, 103, 116
Netherlands 13–14, 15, 32, 98,
107, 133n
Second Dutch War (1665–7)
44
see also navy, Dutch
noblemen 35, 68
noblesse d'épée 93, 104, 106, 111
noblesse de robe 106, 111
North Sea 116

Padfield, P. 22
parliament 16, 31, 39, 83–4, 110,
112, 117–18, 137–8n
Parsons, Talcott 4
Peacock James, 42

Penn, Giles 42
Penn, Admiral William 42
Pepys, Samuel 11, 31, 38, 50, 99,
106, 107, 108, 136n
and Tangier expedition 47
petit état 104–5, 108–9, 110
pirates 38
Plymouth 45, 46, 54
Port St Julian 64
privateering 36, 38, 47, 54, 57, 59,
95, 145n
professions 4–6, 10, 27–30 *see also*
naval profession
psychogenesis 18
pursers 105

Quest for Excitement, The (Elias
and Dunning) 4

Restoration period *see under* navy,
English
rivalry, international 33–4
Rodger, N. A. M. 21
Rooke, Sir George 45
royal mechanism 15–17, 21,
133n
Russell, Admiral Edward, Earl of
Orford 45

Sandwich, Edward Montagu, Earl
of 42
Sarocold, Master John 63, 147n
Sarrazin, Jean 96, 152n
Scotson, John 7
seamen 31
seamen commanders *see* tarpaulin
commanders

ships
  galley fleet 92–3
  increasing size of 34
  man-of-war 37, 40
  rates 37
  sailing, skills needed in 30,
    92–3
Shovel, Admiral Sir Cloudesley
    43, 140–1n
Simmel, Georg 133n
Smith, Captain John 149–50
Smythe, Thomas 43
sociogenesis 18
sociology
  conflict 19–21
  figurational (or process)
    18–19
  military 8–10, 22
  of sport 4, 133n
Spain, *see also under* naval
    profession *and* navy
  government 35, 93–4
  society 12–13, 98–103
status battles 49–51

taboo, 69
tarpaulin (tarred canvas)
    136n
tarpaulin commanders 2, 3,
    36–8, 39, 41–3, 48, 141n
  social origins 40–4
Teitler, G. 8–10, 15, 132–3n

tensions
  axis of 36–40
  group 49–51, 52–3
Terra Australis 54, 57
Thompson, Captain Edward 89
Tilly, Charles 22, 134n
Trinity House 36, 149n

volunteers
  gentlemen 38, 45, 46–7, 56, 71,
    83, 149n
  ship's boys 86–9, 97, 151n

Walsingham, Sir Francis 55, 125,
    146n
Weber, Alfred vii
Weber, Max vii
Weimar Republic vii
William III, king of England
    (1689–1702) *see* William &
    Mary *and under* navy,
    English
William & Mary, king and queen of
    England 21
  see also under navy, English
Wilson, P. A. 4
Winter, John 56, 66, 125
Winter, Sir William, Surveyor of
    the Navy 56
Wouters, Cas 8, 131n

York, Duke of *see* James II